LET IT BE GOOD

Simple Insights for a Satisfied Life

DOM TESTA

Let It Be Good: Simple Insights for a Satisfied Life

By Dom Testa

Copyright © 2025 by Dom Testa/Profound Impact Group, LLC

All rights reserved.

No part of this book may be used, reproduced, or transmitted by any means, electronic or mechanical, including photocopying, recording, or by any information storage and retrieval system, without written permission, except in the case of brief quotations contained within critical articles and reviews. For information, contact the publisher.

Published by Profound Impact Group, LLC

PO Box 506

Alpharetta, GA 30009

ISBN: 978-0-9760564-2-3

Cover design by Damonza

Also by Dom Testa

Non-fiction

Domino On Your Radio: Unlikely Tales From an Introvert on the Air

The Color of Your Dreams: Publish Your Damn Book Already

The Mindbender Book series

The Billy B. Good Fun Facts and Trivia Snacks series

* * *

Fiction

The Eric Swan spy thriller series

The Galahad young adult sci-fi series (written as Tyber North)

The Buster Blank middle grade series (written as Buster Blank)

Wednesday, and Other Dark Tales (written as Harlan Plumber)

* * *

Discover them all at DomTestaBooks.com

Contents

Introduction	ix
1. Let It Be Good	1
2. Wallpaper	9
3. Being Heard	17
4. Two Pins From Perfect	27
5. The Wrong Path	35
6. Just Not Everyone	41
7. Semi-Pro	49
8. Anticipation	57
9. The Cemetery	63
10. Bob Dylan Doesn't Suck	69
11. Paying For It	73
12. A Textured Life	77
13. The Special Occasion	85
14. Celebrating Success	93
15. Passion, Ambition, Perseverance	97
16. Discerning	105
17. Three Magic Words	115
18. The Goldilocks Choice	123
19. Halfway There	131
20. The Gift	141
21. A Remedy for Sadness	149
22. The Positive Password	155
23. Satisfaction	161
24. Closing Thoughts	175
Also by Dom Testa	181

Introduction

The first two people to find out I was writing a book about living a satisfied life had the same reaction.

They laughed. Which doesn't exactly inspire confidence.

One said: "You're a perfectionist. You might be the *last* person who could write about being satisfied."

Hey, no argument with their first comment. I have, indeed, always been the person who constantly pushes for improvement. I'm a staunch opponent of complacency.

I handle criticism well because no one could ever be harder on me than I've been on myself. You could say something shitty about one of my books or about something I said on my radio show and I'd be way ahead of you in noting the defect.

If your goal is to knock me down a few pegs, better roll up your sleeves. I've always been a pro at knocking myself down.

Introduction

It might sound like I've lived a gloomy life. I haven't. I'm quite happy.

But I've always chased *just a little bit better*. If our morning radio show was #1 with a 9.0 share, I wanted #1 with a 9.5. If one of my books reached #1 in an online sales category for two straight weeks, the next one had to be #1 for four weeks.

Having said all that, however, I disagree with the second half of the original observation, when they said: *You might be the last person who could write about being satisfied.*

I'll let you in on a secret. I don't write to teach. I write to learn.

This book took almost two years from start to finish. It involved sifting through scores of articles I've written over the years and blog posts where I seemed to be *close* to learning a valuable lesson.

There were writing trips where I holed up alone for a day or two, stripping away the distracting background noise of life that camouflages the true meaning behind so much of what we experience.

As the months went by, dozens of what I'd thought were just random incidents—acquired throughout a lifetime—fell into place and began to tell a story. Almost like a mosaic of individual life tiles that finally have enough pieces to make a picture clear from a distance.

I gradually recognized how my drive, the thing responsible for my perfectionism, had somehow become more important than the outcome. I'd always assumed I

Introduction

was being graded on the *effort* rather than the finished product. It took decades of processing to understand that you're not "settling" if you try your best and find peace with your limitations.

Now, don't for a moment think this awareness turned me into a slacker. Nor am I advocating that you half-ass your way through life. I am, and will always be, someone who strives for excellence in almost everything, whether it's hosting a morning radio show, writing a novel, or simply painting a wall in the bathroom. I'm wired to give it my all, regardless of the task.

But with age and experience, we *sometimes* achieve wisdom. What I gleaned from my two-year assignment, and what I hope to convey to you, is the realization that sometimes we can just let it be good.

Great is . . . well, great. Great is perhaps the ultimate goal.

Good can be great, too.

My path led me to a plateau where I can now look out over the vast landscape of a life well lived, with all its victories and failures stitched together into some bizarre Picasso-esque quilt. I can see where I took the right trail into the sunshine, and I can also spot where I wandered down a blighted, weed-choked lane of poor decisions. I now appreciate *all* those decisions, even the bad ones that (hopefully) taught me something. I recognize the times I had something wonderful and still wasn't satisfied.

So my friend was wrong; I *am* the right person to

Introduction

write this book because I can, at long last, understand that sometimes you just have to let it be good.

Once I finished my research, I discovered how the concept shows up in a multitude of ways, some obvious, others that produced a revelation.

Like accepting that our woulda/coulda/shoulda thoughts are probably way off (Chapter 7) or how everything we think of as *so important* is really so temporary (Chapter 9) or how social media is our amateurish attempt to "brand" ourselves (Chapter 3).

All these little chunks of life play a bigger role in shaping our happiness and, ultimately, our satisfaction. And Chapter 23 looks at the distinction between those two things.

One last note. You should expect to see yourself in some, if not many, of these chapters. Or, just as likely, you'll spot someone you love, and you'll perhaps understand why they behave the way they do. That understanding can lead to forgiveness, if that's even necessary.

But sometimes the first person we need to forgive is the angst-filled person wearing the manufactured smile in our selfies. The one who always questions if they or their actions are good enough.

You—and they—probably are.

Chapter 1
Let It Be Good

On a vacation to New England, my wife and I discovered an outdoor bar that truly kicked ass. Vermont is gorgeous to begin with, and we happened to be there on a perfect autumn afternoon, with blue skies and warm temperatures.

As much as I enjoy a nice bar, it's not often I gush over them. This particular establishment sat on gently sloping property behind a restaurant, overlooking a small river. Towering shade trees, just beginning to tease the technicolor show they'd soon put on in force, provided respite from the sun. The drinks were moderately priced, the food interesting and well-prepared, and the service impeccable.

For what it's worth, the bar was ergonomically perfect, too. Just the right depth to the tabletop—not too skinny, not too wide—at a comfortable height, and with foot rests positioned just where they need to be. You may or may not understand exactly how all that matters. We are "eat at the bar" people. It matters.

The two hours flew by as we enjoyed appetizers and cocktails. We got to know some of the locals who were, to our astonishment, pleasant and welcoming. Look, the astonishment is no slam against Vermonters, who, I'm sure, are good, salt-of-the-Earth people. They're just, at least in my experience, *different*. A few degrees off-kilter. And not exactly known for embracing outsiders with open arms.

On this day, however, we must've stumbled across the exceptions. Laughs were plentiful. They even treated us to some local gossip. Of course, we had no idea who the subjects of these stories were, but somehow that made the gossip even sweeter. Our imaginations were free to go off canvas and paint any picture we wanted.

It was such a fun experience. When we left, we said, *This was so cool. Let's come back tomorrow night.*

We did.

And it was utterly disappointing.

The weather was still nice, but the appetizers weren't nearly as good, the new bartender was snobby, and the overall atmosphere was flat. Our company on this evening displayed the stand-offish personality I alluded to above. More than once we leaned in close to each other and wondered how, from one day to the next, it could be so different.

We paid the tab and left after an hour. Walking back to the car, both of us now quiet, my wife and I absorbed this let-down. During our drive back to the bed-and-breakfast, I finally uttered the words that summed up the two extreme experiences:

Why didn't we just let it be good?

How many times do we take something that's *good* and try to unnaturally replicate it or somehow make it even *better*? We're eager for that same dopamine hit, I suppose.

We should just let it be good.

I've had a lot of time since my trek through Vermont and Maine to not only bask in the beauty I witnessed in nature, but to contemplate an interesting quirk of *human* nature. What drives our pursuit of the repeat performance?

My first thought was that most of us have so much routine baked into our lives that anything extraordinary cries out for more. Sorta like eating one Oreo or one Dorito—your brain stubbornly informs you that one is not enough. It's possible Gretchen and I knew our vacation was winding down and we wanted one more injection of the good life before sliding back into normal daily life.

But eventually I rejected the notion. There are just too many other instances where that explanation doesn't apply.

Case in point: Not long ago, I posted a photo on social media of a T-shirt my son sported one day when we met up for lunch. It featured a cartoonish drawing of an old-school computer floppy disk, a VHS tape, and a cassette, all holding hands. The caption read: *Never Forget*.

Okay, that's just funny. It's succinct, silly, and sentimental. I had to post the photo online to share the humor.

And then came the torrent of comments, including:

Why doesn't it have a vinyl album?
What about an 8-track tape? I don't see an 8-track.
Hey, why no CDs? Those are old-fashioned now, too, you know.

Sigh. I wanted to respond to each of these: *Let it be good. Just let it be good.*

Not everything has to be one-upped. Or, like my visit to the pleasant outdoor bar, not everything has to be duplicated. Sometimes we should just enjoy every ounce of an experience, squeeze the ever-loving joy out of it, and let it be the good experience it was meant to be. Then move on.

I know social media thrives on comments, and sometimes seems to demand it. (An upcoming chapter explores the weirdness of social media.) But this photo of my son's shirt could've easily stood alone, with merely a thumbs-up or laughing emoji as a response. That would've sufficed. We all would've shared a chuckle and scrolled on.

But rarely will you find a funny post that doesn't attract the people who must refine. Or attempt an improvement. This particular shirt needed neither. Yeah, *sometimes* it's good fun to keep a joke rolling, but I submit it may often be better to just absorb it in all its goddamned goodness.

For most creative people, this is something of a curse because we tend to never be satisfied with our creations. Paintings, stories, craftwork, or any other artistic endeavor—we look past something simple and good, and we long to make it spectacular.

But simple and good often *are* spectacular. Sometimes much more so because of the simplicity.

It took that September trip to a small-town bar in Vermont for me to become conscious of my attempts to replicate or embellish good experiences again and again in my life. Hey, sometimes it works out. Many times, however, it's a big letdown.

Later—because I actually enjoy exploring the origins of our funny human idiosyncrasies—I began wondering if this was a symptom of some other, more easily definable characteristic. And the one that popped into my head straight away was:

Never being satisfied.

Good lord, that couldn't really be true, could it? Suddenly, what struck me as an amusing observation took on a different quality altogether. By the time I got home a few days later, I'd read multiple pieces on this element of our personalities, trying to see if it at least applied to me, if not the population in general.

And . . . I think it might.

Later in this book, you'll find a chapter on the difficulties some people have when it comes to celebrating success. But to boil it down, they constantly compare themselves and their work to others—I can hear Ned Ryerson from the movie *"Groundhog Day"* saying "*Bing*!"—and they can often be perfectionists.

Bing again!

One paper on the subject mentioned a distaste for settling. In that respect, see the upcoming chapter titled "Discerning." It might sound like it contradicts what I'm endorsing in this book. You might think: *Wait, Dom, you tell us to let it be good—and then you tell us something's not good enough?*

Well . . . yeah. It still has to be *good* before you can let it be that way. A satisfied life doesn't mean a life of settling for substandard, simply in order to get along. It's more about holding back the demons that demand *perfection*, the ones that constantly want you to one-up every nice thing that tumbles into your lap.

I'm not too proud to admit my flaws. I recognize I'm hard on myself, that I hold myself and others to higher standards, and I'm constantly striving to improve. These traits don't make me a bad person. In fact, in many respects, I'd say these characteristics have driven the bulk of my successes across three careers simultaneously.

But I've learned a lot over the years about that line between good and perfection. I'm still a student of life, studying the quirks and mind games that can hold us back from a satisfied life.

What about you? Are you able to patiently see the

goodness in everyday life? Can you appreciate it? Or do you constantly try to improve what's already good in the first place?

An old French proverb, made famous by Voltaire, claimed that perfect is the enemy of good. It's been twisted a few different ways, yet it still boils down to the idea that demanding perfection is no way to live. If you're as guilty of it as I am, then this is not a news flash.

Imagine how much pressure we'd eliminate from our lives if we unhooked the engine from the perfection train. If we learned to enjoy that wonderful night at the quaint Vermont bar, then set out the next day for an entirely new—and who knows, perhaps an equally glorious—experience.

Yes, life might deal us a rough hand from time to time, but it doles out its share of good, too. When you recognize that, it's important to draw from your reservoir of gratitude rather than to immediately hunt for a replica.

I know this for sure: There are only so many antiquated pieces of technology that could've made my son's T-shirt perfect, and the number was three. Any more and it's cluttered and suffocated.

Our lives are like the shirt. On a daily basis, we're gifted good experiences, some big, some small. The next time you're blessed, find the point of perfect satiation and walk away.

Let it be good.

Chapter 2
Wallpaper

The bed-and-breakfast sat about a mile from the historic City Centre of Canterbury, tucked into a modern suburb of the 2,000-year-old British town. A mile turned out to be the perfect distance; one could find a peaceful night's sleep outside the hubbub of the action, but get in a pleasant walk when it was time to explore.

On a morning with crystal clear blue skies and with a backpack slung over one shoulder, I crossed a pedestrian bridge over the A28 and approached a stunning sight. Looming before me, stark, gray stone walls encircled the city. But these were not just any old walls. They were originally built by the Romans, just before the year 300. Over the centuries, there have been long stretches of time when they fell into disrepair, only to later be reinforced and/or rebuilt.

What captivated me, besides their antiquity, was just how large and stout they were. In some places, an original Roman section can still stand 16 feet tall, while in other spots they reach nearly 20 feet. At the base, they can be as much as seven feet thick. During the peak of Roman control, there were two dozen large towers spaced out around the circumference of the town, some of these rising as tall as a seven-story building.

I stood transfixed, staring at these walls that date back more than 1,700 years. They appeared forbidding in some respects, possibly because they were erected by a mighty army representing one of the most fearsome and dominant empires the world has ever seen. And yet, after closer observation, I could see they'd also softened over time, the result of weather and the distress of modern pollution.

But still eye-popping.

And that's the other thing that struck me. As I stood on that bridge, gazing upon this remarkable history, a mad procession of cars sped past below me. It was loud, this rumbling rush of humanity, the speed blurring the drivers' faces as they hurried past, on their way to another appointment or scurrying into work, beginning what likely was another ordinary day.

Sipping some water, I looked back and forth between the wall and the traffic, wondering:

Do the people racing along even know these walls are here? How can they not be completely mesmerized by the staggering history of it all?

A few hours later, sitting at a table outside a quaint pub called The Old Buttermarket—having now switched from water to lager—I chatted with a local named Devon and I floated those same questions to him.

"Well," he said with a crooked smile. "It's like this. Ya say you're from Colorado, right? I 'spose you don't notice the Rocky Mountains anymore, do ya?"

Then he lifted a pint to his lips and we both took a moment to savor his wisdom.

Immediately, I flashed back to a previous trip to another city rich in ancient history. In fact, the very birthplace of the empire that had built the Canterbury walls: Rome.

It had been a long, hot summer day, and I was ready for an evening of good food and even better wine. But there was still one more thing I wanted to experience before winding down. I'd spent hours at the Vatican, had gazed in awe at the ceiling of the Sistine Chapel, and had one more historical prize to take in before calling it a day.

I trudged up the steps from the bowels of one of Rome's subway stations and there it was: the legendary Colosseum, more magnificent in person than any pictures or travel documentary could paint it. Not just its massive size, but the innate feeling of power and majesty still oozing from the stones.

This monument to the strength and authority of the mighty Roman Empire loomed overhead, all two thousand years of its grandeur on display. You could almost hear echoes from the roars of 50,000 spectators watching the gladiatorial games.

Well, *almost* hear them is right; those echoes were drowned out by the parade of vehicles whizzing past, a combination of cars, trucks, buses, and Italian motorbikes. Beyond the traffic, I swept my gaze across fast-food restaurants, pharmacies, and dry cleaners flanking the legendary Colosseum.

Again, I had to wonder if the residents had almost forgotten the ruins were even there. Did the old guy manning the bustling newsstand across the street ever look up and truly absorb the glory of Emperor Vespasian's handiwork? Or had this colossal stone wonder merely become . . . wallpaper?

I don't know why the experiences in Canterbury and Rome bothered me. I guess it seemed as if the ancient relics were somehow disrespected. I know that's not the case, but I couldn't get over the feeling, regardless.

The truth is, most people usually travel with a tangible purpose: to visit friends, to sightsee, to experience new cultures. For some, however, the goal is to simply fulfill a wish list. Another pub patron I chatted with in Canterbury, a teacher from Wales named Paul, put it succinctly: "People just go places to tick them off a list. They have no reason for doing it other than to say they did."

Or, I thought silently, to collect photos to impress friends on social media. *Look what I did! Look what I saw!*

That's a cynical way to look at it, but Paul and I are not far off in our assessments. And if that's why you travel, who am I to question your primary goal?

Side note: I hope when you visit some of these ancient wonders that you at least try to show a bit of respect. It took every ounce of self-control for me to not throttle the brutish American I overheard at Stonehenge saying, "Pfft. A bunch of rocks. We drove all the way out here for *this*?"

Dumbass. Go home.

Sorry, I still bristle when I think of it.

The reason for this chapter, the primary takeaway, and the thing that dominated my thoughts for the rest of that trip to England, had more to do with an *intangible* benefit of the vacation. Because regardless of the original intent, our travels deliver something of immense value beyond the photos and the memories.

We hopefully recognize what has become our *own* wallpaper.

Devon, the salty local outside that pub in Canterbury, was exactly right. At the time of my getaway, I'd had the stately Rocky Mountains as a backdrop for almost thirty years, and I had to admit there were days when I never saw them. Oh, they may have radiated through my windshield on a daily basis, but I'd become numb to the purple mountain majesties spread out before me.

No different than those commuters in Canterbury who were blind to a sixteen-foot stone wall that's embraced their city for nearly two millennia.

There's no shame in this—we simply become oblivious to things around us over time, whether it's a mountain range, a medieval cathedral, or—unfortunately—a loved one. The truth is, we're stimulated on a regular basis by an overwhelming influx of new data, new images, features and products vying for our attention, and we lose sight of the majesty of a Colosseum. Or a person.

What has become wallpaper in *your* world? People who live along Colorado's Front Range undoubtedly grow anesthetized to the mountain views. Folks who spend day in and day out with the crashing waves of a glorious rocky coastline probably go weeks without really noticing it.

On a simpler note, some might have a home way out in the sticks, far from the light pollution pumped out by major cities, and yet they rarely stop and look up at the glittering wonder of the Milky Way.

Even worse, we get so desensitized by our daily routines that the people around us become a sort of living wallpaper. We notice that they're around, we even go so far as to carry on dialogue with them—but we don't really *see* them every day. It's not unusual for some people to change their hairstyle—maybe even their hair *color*—and their family or friends don't even notice.

Or we blink and our children have gone from diapers to graduating.

I discovered that a change of scenery can revive our sense of wonder and gratitude. As a vigorous advocate of solo travel for many years, I wrote a piece about the subject that was hailed by Yahoo Travel because it pointed out all the things you're more likely to see and experience when you're not traveling with another person.

Not only do these solo excursions help us see sights that might teach us appreciation for the beauty of our environment back home, but they might also produce a healthy dose of longing for the people we've recently taken for granted.

Travel as more than just a way to collect social media style points.

Travel as a *life reboot*.

When I landed at Denver International Airport after ten days in the U.K., I stood at the end of the concourse and gazed out the floor-to-ceiling windows.

At my glorious wallpaper.

Chapter 3
Being Heard

Social media speaks to us because we're social beings. I have no idea what Mark Zuckerberg or the Winklevoss twins *really* thought about the social experiment that turned into Facebook, and I don't know if they were truly visionaries when it came to how we're socially wired as a species. But damn, whether you like it or not, nothing has ever tapped into the human psyche the way social media has since the mid-2000s.

I have to laugh at the fact people use social media to blast social media. Rarely a week goes by that someone doesn't post, "This has become way too toxic. So I'm out."

They probably don't see the irony in their message.

If you think I'm going to devote this chapter to how social media steals our happiness and stomps it into a lifeless pulp, you're wrong.

If you think I'm going to talk about how the algorithms are designed to bring out the very worst in us, nope.

If you think I'm going to lecture you about how the world's most powerful people (in tech) are manipulating our emotions—especially anger—to make a buck . . . I'm not going to do that, either.

I believe all three of those things are true. But that's not what this chapter is about.

Between July 2022 and July 2023, I went 371 days between posts on Facebook. There was no big announcement. I just checked out. No, I'm not some sort of evangelist, preaching that we all must abandon the evils of social media. I just took a break without telling anyone.

As one popular meme puts it: "You're not an airline. No need to announce your departure."

The result of my social media vacation? Well, I can say for a fact that my stress levels declined. There was an odd feeling of freedom to not feel pressure to stay dialed in.

And when I did start posting again, I never checked back in to see how many people "liked" my posts. About every other day I'd log in to respond to comments—I've heard to not do that is rude—but that was it. I went at least two years without scrolling through other content at all.

Am I a superior being? No, that's not what this is about.

It's that I finally learned, after having social media

accounts for 14 years, what the platforms are actually doing *for* us and what they're doing *to* us.

My life is different from the average person's. I host a morning radio show with a shit-ton of listeners. I have my own platform, I guess you could say, weekday mornings for four hours a day. If there's something I want to say to a large audience, I merely have to crack open the microphone and talk.

But the average person has no platform, other than the ones we know as Facebook, Instagram, TikTok, Twitter/X, Pinterest, and others. That's how the average person reaches a mass audience.

As someone once told me, "Facebook is *'People'* magazine for the average person." It's their one chance to be noticed. To be a star.

I'm working on a screenplay, a story I've nurtured for several years. The script's basic idea is that most people go their entire lives without really being heard by anyone. And the allure of people actually listening to what you have to say is magnetic.

Since—as I write this—I've been on the radio for nearly half a century, I've become used to the idea that my words are broadcast to a large audience. And, just as important, I get immediate feedback from that audience.

But the average person? They would get up in the morning, they'd worry about the state of the world or their own life, they'd trudge to work, then back home, before starting the whole process over the next day. If they had anything to say about the state of that world, there was no one to listen to them.

Then, in 2004, this thing called Facebook popped up. In just a few years, it spread like a virus around the world. And why? Because it offered people an opportunity to be heard. Hey, maybe only 20 people would see your comment, but that was more than most people were used to. They usually had only the same two or three coworkers in the office break room who were cornered into listening to their rants.

Social media is not about sharing funny cat memes—although I love those. No, social media is a drug. Our body has a powerful reaction to any jolt of dopamine, the chemical messenger that's released when you have feelings of pleasure or accomplishment. We grow to crave those jolts, which is where the drug metaphor comes into play. Post something on social media, and every time someone clicks "like" or chooses a heart emoji, it tickles your reward center. You get high.

It's why posting something on Facebook is only half the game. After that, most people check back in—some log in every few minutes—to get that dopamine blast when someone likes the post or adds a comment. They have found their tribe. They have connected. And, if the gods are smiling upon them, the social media algorithm notices and pushes that post to hundreds or thousands more, ultimately enhancing the cycle and delivering more of a rush.

In case you haven't heard it shouted from the mountaintops, social media platforms are truly playing us. Specifically, they're toying with our emotions. And since that chemical release brings you back again and again, the platforms can place more eyeballs on their advertisements. You get high, they get rich.

Then there's yet another component: For the first time in history, people have their own version of a PR machine at their disposal.

What most people *really* are doing with social media is creating an image of themselves they want to project to the world. Back in the day, only celebrities and politicians had the resources to mold an image for the public. The average person had no control over their personal narrative.

Today? Some people spend several hours a week, every week, fabricating a look and an image. And they do it in several ways:

- Taking dozens of selfies and critically eliminating any that don't produce the best look. Then, running the surviving pics through filter after filter.

- Posting photos and experiences that display the life they want people to believe they enjoy on a daily basis. This could be vacation photos, shots from concerts and festivals, and luxurious dinners out.

- Posting or sharing memes and billboards advocating a social or political position, purely a showcase for their 'values.'

And many more, obviously. But the underlying motivation is to craft a positive image, an avatar one can be proud of.

Social media, in other words, is nothing more than a personal public relations tool.

Is this wrong? Is it bad? Depends on how you look at it. I would maintain it's certainly not an honest portrayal.

But neither was your senior photo from high school. I'll bet you rarely, if ever, looked like that picture. Yet that was what you chose to represent you to the world.

The funny thing is, we all know this is true—and yet it changes nothing. I know what's generally posted is bullshit, you know what's generally posted is bullshit, and we all agree to just smile and nod and embrace the bullshit.

In the grand scheme of things, it probably doesn't hurt anything. It's just a quirky, funny side to our human design.

So, to go back to my earlier point: No, this is not me screaming that everyone needs to wean themselves from the beast. Besides, people have been sounding the alarm about social media for more than a decade and hardly anyone is paying attention. I certainly don't expect my book to miraculously change a cultural paradigm.

What I *do* hope to accomplish, however, is to simply point out that Facebook and other similar platforms succeed because people are desperate to project a solid image, and to be heard. And, strange as it may be, people want to be heard even if they don't have anything of real substance to say. Just offering their own little comment to someone else's post is often enough. *Just hear me out*, they're saying. *My voice counts.*

Perhaps it's because we're at a point where we finally understand that the people we elect to speak for us aren't really speaking for us anymore—if they ever have. Or our so-called role models have proven they're no more qualified to be a spokesperson than anyone else.

Or maybe we just feel like very small fish in a super-sized pond, and we're tired of being invisible.

Over the last 20 years, we've all basically been fumbling through the infant and adolescent stages of this new technology. We've been test subjects, guinea pigs for the tech giants as they learned how to profit from our human tendencies. And we've happily provided the data for them because we lusted for the dopamine. That's the currency they use to pay us.

To me, the best lesson we can take from this has nothing to do with whether or not social media is *good* or *bad*. The lesson/question is: Does social media truly bring you satisfaction? When you post something and the same 14 people like it, and the same five people treat you to a comment—does that *really* fulfill you?

Or are you subsisting on tiny little chemical spurts, getting by until the next post and the next injection?

And some of those chemical spurts, it must be pointed out, aren't always positive. It's been proposed that the big platforms are built to encourage negative responses. I won't argue that one way or the other.

However, what I *do* believe is that it's not just a post

that goes viral. I think something that ignites your anger provides fuel for your thoughts to go *internally* viral, too. We stew on something we saw on social media, letting it hijack what might've been, at one point, a good day.

And your interactions in this viral world can often escalate, showcasing your worst tendencies in an exponential manner. People who, in person, would never say something vile to another human being find themselves going a little crazy when the internet is involved. In some ways, it's not even real, but rather an outcome of your viral mind.

The fallout, however, can—and often is—*very* real. Think of the people who normally are good, decent folks, but who lost their shit on X or Facebook or TikTok, and then suffered the consequences from social judgment.

When you examine it, are those brief snippets of engagement bringing you genuine happiness? Or is it possible you're just trapped on the social merry-go-round, a lather-rinse-repeat cycle that has become the very definition of rote: mechanical and repetitious?

If you can find one or two friends with whom you can actually sit down and have a face-to-face conversation, I promise you'll be heard way more than anything you could post online. The huge platforms are now a swarm of white noise. The "connection" you're making is mostly artificial. In his book *Stolen Focus,* author

Johann Hari refers to social media connections as "hollow parodies of friendship."

That's one of the best descriptions I've heard.

Sure, the convenience factor is what keeps people coming back for more, not much different than how the convenience of fast food keeps people from quality nutrition. It's just easier.

Social media is easier. A "like" button and a bag of chicken nuggets provide the same dopamine hit.

When it comes to a satisfied life, I guess it's a matter of how much *real* you value, compared to how much artificial/convenient?

And only you can make those decisions.

Chapter 4
Two Pins From Perfect

On a Saturday afternoon in May 2011, I went bowling and connected with the universe. That's right, I found enlightenment wearing rented shoes, one of those light-bulb moments tossed our way from time to time. Usually we're so distracted we miss it altogether, but on this day I was tuned in.

To be clear, I'm not a regular bowler. I maybe get out once every couple of years, just to have some fun with friends. I'm certainly no pro. I don't own my own ball, nor my own pair of bowling shoes. Count on me to grab a pitted 15-pound ball off the rack and wind up with a score in the 130-140 range, which is not bad, I think.

But on this particular May afternoon, I channeled something. It was one of those days that comes along when you least expect it, as if the gods have randomly chosen that space and time to smile upon you.

In other words, I was on fire.

I started the game with a strike. Always a fun way to

begin, and guaranteed to elicit hoots and hollers from your playing partners, with sarcastic shouts of "He's a ringer!" Everyone had a good laugh, I took a sip of my beer, and waited for my next turn.

That was another strike. Then I rolled a third one. Now there was genuine laughter in my little group of four, because hacks like me never start a game with a turkey. That's three strikes in a row, if you don't know bowler lingo.

Next time up: another strike.

In fact, I rolled a strike in the first six frames. The bowling alley was packed that day, and the people on the surrounding lanes heard the commotion and were now suddenly paying very close attention to what I was doing.

Did it fluster me? Apparently not, because I proceeded to roll strikes in the seventh and eighth frames, too. This brought still more laughter from my friends, and polite applause from the onlookers.

Eight strikes in a row to start the game. *This is ridiculous*, we all said. *The bowling gods are smiling. I'm unconscious. I'm the new Earl Anthony* (an old-time professional bowler, and, like me, a lefty).

For the first time, as I gazed at the endless string of X's on the electronic scoreboard above my head, I wondered:

Could I bowl a 300? I mean, really . . . could I?

Gliding down the approach for the ninth frame, I felt calm. I released the dull, chipped ball, it hooked directly into the pocket, a thing of beauty, a sure ninth strike.

The pins scattered, the crowd cheered, and . . . the ten pin remained standing.

Somehow, in that maelstrom of swirling bowling pins, one soldier refused to fall. I grinned as I turned around to a standing ovation from the crowd.

I'm proud to say I picked up the spare.

Oh, but wait. Tenth frame, another strike. Then another one.

On the third ball of the frame, my final fling, that same ten pin refused to budge. Out of twelve attempts, I'd made ten strikes, along with a nine and a nine. In case you're wondering, that adds up to a score of 278.

Until this moment, my highest score ever had been a 205 or 210, something like that. This was insane.

I still have the printed scoresheet, dated and signed by the others in my group, a reminder that on this one day I was two pins from perfect.

So let's talk about that.

I've always maintained there's no such thing as a perfect 10. Many disagree, but I believe the scale should stop at 9.9, a breath away from the pinnacle. Perhaps it's an element of my personality, maybe some consequence of the way I was raised. But I'm uncomfortable with the idea that we ever achieve *perfection*.

No matter how successful I am at any of my endeavors—and I have my fingers into a lot of stuff—I never, ever want to feel like I've mastered anything. To me, there should always be room for improvement.

This concept does not sit well with everyone, and I accept that. Some people believe with all their heart that perfection is attainable; some claim they've actually reached it in certain areas of their life.

When the judges on *"Dancing With The Stars"* hand out perfect 10s to contestants, some will nod and agree it couldn't possibly have been any better. But really? There was *nothing* the dancer could have done better? Not one move a little more graceful, not one step that couldn't be tweaked a tad?

Was that absolute *perfection* on the dance floor, or just a way to goose the crowd and drum up artificial enthusiasm for the people at home, sitting on their butts, watching others perform?

There clearly are two schools of thought on this. I don't know if I've ever considered anything "perfect," and might go so far as to say nothing can ever be perfect.

Then I read John Green's tremendous book called "The Anthropocene Reviewed." In it, he discussed sunsets. At one point he said to NOT give something five stars because "nothing is perfect" is bullshit.

Okay, this made me laugh. And I'll concede his point when it comes to sunsets.

And I'll throw in peanut butter, too. That's perfect.

Call me a nitpicking hard-ass, if you must. But I believe in my heart that, as much as I tried on that bowling alley, the universe was confirming that I'm doing things the right way. For me, anyway.

Let It Be Good

I was two pins from perfect that Saturday afternoon, because I always—*always*—need to feel like there's still one more step to climb, one more skill to refine, one more talent to develop. I hate the idea of a perfect score.

Hey, in the introduction of this book I acknowledged that I can be very critical of myself. But I don't think it manifests in a grumpy way. Whether it was something about my upbringing or just an odd strand of my DNA, I'm constantly driven to be a little bit better.

I heard an interesting interview with Dr. Anna Lembke, a psychiatrist who pioneered some fascinating discoveries into the role that dopamine plays in our lives, particularly regarding addiction. Dopamine, if you're not sure, is a neurotransmitter in our brains—basically a chemical messenger—that plays an important role in many of our day-to-day functions. We know it mostly through its connection to our system of reward and motivation. You often hear people talk about getting a burst of dopamine when they experience something that brings them joy.

Dr. Lembke said something that made me hit pause during the podcast so I could stop and think. She talked about how, when we come off a dopamine high, our body overcompensates the other direction, so we actually feel either a strong desire for something or we feel down and depressed. Our brain, looking for a measure of balance, wants to then repeat the thing that brought such feelings of happiness in the first place.

It explains a lot about addiction, that's for sure,

whether it's alcohol, drugs, food, sex, shopping, or whatever.

And Lembke says we evolved this way because our earliest ancestors, as hunters, *needed* that drive to keep searching for more. They couldn't just sit around and congratulate themselves all day for a great job finding food because that food would soon run out. They had to push on for more.

As she said, "It's made us the ultimate seekers."

I think that might explain, at least in part, my overactive desire to be better or to constantly improve some element of my life. Perhaps it's simply my body chemistry pushing me more than the average person. That's not better or worse; it's just different. It also could explain why some people are more easily satisfied while others strive for more, whether it's in sports, business, or having the best yard in the neighborhood.

Dopamine affects almost every aspect of our lives, so it really depends on our own personal wiring. Your body's relationship with this and other chemical processes will certainly differ from everyone else.

Did I try to get that 300 at the bowling alley? Of course I did! I gave it all I had, and I'm telling you that goddamned ball was right in the pocket both times I failed to get a strike.

But rather than throwing something in disgust at that ten pin—the one that mocked me twice in what otherwise would have been perfection—I found laughter and inspiration.

So as you finish this chapter, you're probably either nodding in agreement with me because you're the same way, or you're shaking your head, thinking I must live a tormented life. I promise you I don't.

Maybe it's just a quirky way of dodging complacency.

My morning radio show has had countless ratings periods where we were #1 in the most important demographics. Many people would be satisfied. Me? I celebrated briefly, then looked ahead to the next ratings period, searching for ways to make the show even better. Like those ancestral hunters, trudging back to the hunting ground with their spears.

To me, coming in first place doesn't mean you're perfect. I noticed that Michael Phelps didn't take his first *twenty* Olympic gold medals and go home. He kept diving back into that pool, doing everything he could to shave another tenth-of-a-second off his best time. Does that make *him* miserable?

One thing you'll note about this episode is that I'm not advocating for anyone else to be this way. We're all uniquely wired. We might share many similar traits, but there are a lot of shades on the color wheel.

I just happen to have a trait that scorns complacency, hates the idea of quitting while I'm ahead, and completely rejects the idea that any dancer ever scored a PERFECT 10.

And here's one last thought about this idea of perfection:

It's possible most of us would never want perfection anyway because it takes all the fun and joy out of the event.

Think about it. If every time you went bowling you rolled a strike in every frame, you'd celebrate like crazy—at first. But eventually there'd be no fun in it at all. Remove the challenge and you remove the joy of the test.

Today, when you walk into my basement, you're greeted by an oversized and fashionably decorated bowling pin, a gift from one of my bowling partners that day. It's my fun reminder that we can tip-toe up to perfection, we can flirt with what we call *the best*, and we can acknowledge that we've done very, very well.

But on some level, I know being two pins from perfect keeps complacency at bay.

Chapter 5
The Wrong Path

Thought-a-Day calendars are cheesy. I've never bought one—but I received one as a Christmas gift from Susan, the wonderful, sweet woman who cleaned my house twice a month.

You know how these calendars work, right? They have 365 individual pages, and each morning you tear off the last one, throw it away, then read the deep thought for the new day. Sometimes I'd forget for a week at a time, then have to play catchup. But I *always* made sure that daily-thought calendar was up to date on the days Susan came in.

I never told her this, obviously, but almost all the deep thoughts on those five-inch-by-five-inch pages produced an eye roll from me. (Today's thought: *You CAN do it!*)

Seriously, as a writer, it chapped my ass thinking that somebody was squirreled away at a desk somewhere, writing or even just compiling these horrible Thought-a-

Day calendars, and probably making more than I did from my book sales. Grrr!

And come on, it's not like it would take long. I'll bet this person could crank out a month's worth before lunch.

Monday: "*Your life is in nobody's hands but yours.*"
Tuesday: "*You only discover a true friend when your soul is having a cloudy day.*"

I just made those up in about 15 seconds, and I swear that's the stuff I saw in my kitchen each morning as I tore off a new page. It was dreck.

Until one day it wasn't.

On a random Thursday in August, I tore off the preceding page to find this:

No matter how far you've traveled down the wrong path, turn back.

For the first time in the roughly 220 days I'd done this routine, I stood in my kitchen, staring down at the deep thought. In fact, I must've looked at that page for a full minute, thinking. Then I thought about it on the drive to work.

And, when I got home later, I looked at it again. There was something about this message I couldn't shake.

The next morning, I did something I hadn't done

before. After tearing it off, instead of throwing it in the trash, I preserved the thoughtful page—credited, by the way, as a Turkish proverb—on the bulletin board behind my desk. It stayed there for nearly ten years, coming down only because I moved. It wound up in a box, but I still have it.

The proverb is both simple and profound—hell, for all I know that may be the very definition of a proverb. But this particular sentence, in only 12 words, had an enormous impact on me.

At the time, I was involved in a personal relationship I had no business being in. You've probably been there at least once. I'd known it for quite a while, but was reluctant to end it for one ridiculous reason: I'd invested so much time and effort.

I feel you nodding through the ether.

Your rational brain is telling you the relationship is not right, but you hesitate to pull the plug. I was that big dummy who kept stubbornly believing the other person would change, that we just had to keep weathering the bumpy seas and it would all smooth out in the end.

There was *no way* it would smooth out. At the time I read that calendar page, I'd spent at least a full year longer than I should've with this person.

Many times it's not a personal relationship, but a professional one. You've been at a job for so long that it seems crazy to throw it away and start over again somewhere else. All that seniority, all those benefits, all that accrued time off, and on and on. You seem to make up a new excuse to *not* leave every time the idea occurs to you.

A chunk of your brain informs you that you'd be an idiot to walk out the door. So you don't.

What's wrong with us? I'll tell you what I think:

It's a pride issue.

We add up all the months and years we've put into a personal or professional relationship and we resist making a change simply because we hate to feel like a failure. You've heard of throwing good money after bad. Well, we also throw good *years* after bad.

Granted, in some cases the hesitation is warranted. Many times you simply need a minor step back, a chance to breathe. I would never advocate blowing up a relationship just because you're in a temporary trough. Hopefully you recognize when it's just a brief, tough patch.

Sometimes, though, you *know* you're trudging down the wrong path. Everything screams that you need to make a change, but you won't pull the trigger. Maybe you don't want to give up because it will somehow—at least in your mind—invalidate everything you've built.

Maybe you're just plain scared. No shame in that, my friend.

Turning around on that path is hard, maybe one of the hardest things we'll ever do. We're afraid of how things will turn out, or how others will be affected. But let me assure you: If it's the right thing to do, the sooner you do it, the better. All you're doing now is marching farther and farther away from the *right* path, and you have only so many years to soak up the happiness and satisfaction that comes from being where you need to be.

Let It Be Good

Maybe it's because of my long history in radio, but I often find myself thinking in song lyrics. In the mid-1970s, Diana Ross had a number one hit (written by Michael Masser and Gerry Goffin) that spoke to me when I thought about living life on the wrong path. She sang:

Do you know where you're going to?
Do you like the things that life is showing you?

That Turkish proverb was like a neon sign flashing before my eyes: I didn't like the things that life was showing me. And it was *my* choice. I was the one choosing to stay on the wrong path.

After sleeping on it for a week, I ended the rocky relationship. And, perhaps no surprise, all the fear and worry turned out to be for naught. It wound up being one of the best decisions I've ever made. My new path brought me back into the sunshine.

And, to toss in another old reference: In the movie "*City Slickers,*" Billy Crystal's wife tells him:

"Go and find your smile."

There's a good chance your smile is waiting back at the trailhead, right there at the turnoff where you started your trek down the wrong path. The one you know is wrong for you.

Give some thought today to your own path. Is it the one you're supposed to be walking? Is it bringing you the joy you should be experiencing?

To quote more of that Diana Ross song:

Why must we wait so long before we'll see
How sad the answers to those questions can be?

Each step down that path is time you won't get back. Is today the day you push aside the fear and plot a new heading?

Take a deep breath, and just remind yourself:

It's not a failure. It's a course correction.

Chapter 6
Just Not Everyone

Stories have the power to help us understand concepts, which is why our early ancestors began telling them around campfires. For this chapter, I actually have two stories.

You'll have to provide your own campfire.

Michelle agonized over the decision for weeks. It hadn't even been her idea in the first place, which contributed to the waffling she now experienced. One day she was sure it was the right thing to do, the next day it was the dumbest thing she'd ever contemplated.

Finally, she summoned her courage, made an appointment, and the stylist she'd seen for 13 years lopped off most of Michelle's hair. Altered the color a bit, too. It was an entirely new look for her. A fresh start. A bold new beginning.

All the uncertainty she'd felt evaporated when she

posted a photo and the comments were all glowing. Then she began showing up at gatherings of friends, and everyone loved the change, gushing over how gorgeous she looked with the new 'do. More than one asked for the name and number of her stylist. Michelle could not be more thrilled. She wondered why she'd hesitated so long.

Oh, but wait. Did I say *everyone* loved the change?

Sitting in the stands at her daughter's volleyball game, another mom—more an acquaintance than a friend—struck up a conversation about the new look. Michelle said the woman actually squinted while appraising it, as if she was about to render an opinion on a priceless work of art.

Then she told Michelle: "You know, I almost did the same thing last year. Then I realized it would actually make me look older. So I kept the long hair. Good for you for going for it, though."

And that was all it took. No matter how many people complimented her afterwards, no matter how many online comments included hearts and the hug emoji, she focused on one thought:

Now I look old.

Ben had never shown an interest in books or reading until he reached college. Until that point, it had always seemed like "an assignment," something he was forced to do for school. Reading for enjoyment had honestly never even occurred to him.

In his sophomore year, however, he picked up his

roommate's tattered copy of "*Into Thin Air*," Jon Krakauer's emotionally charged account of his experience during an ascent of Mount Everest, an expedition that turned deadly.

Ben was riveted. When he finished, he did what many people do. He sought out another book by the same author. Within a week, he'd finished "*Into The Wild*."

From that point on, he never stopped reading, branching out from nonfiction to fiction, absorbing it all. It was like he'd been a man dying of thirst and now took in the gush of water from a fire hose.

And, like many before him, his sudden discovery of books made him stop and think: *Maybe I should try writing something.*

That's what he did. And, to his surprise, he found he had a knack for it. As one person commented after reading one of his early attempts, "You've got a real flair for compelling language."

He sat down and began filling a blank screen with that compelling language. Page after page. Some days the words came easily, and some days he struggled to finish two sentences.

But he never gave up.

Two years later, he self-published his first book. No, it didn't sell very many copies, but he'd poured his heart and soul into it, and the early reviews were mostly kind.

That's not a given, by the way. Online reviews, since they're primarily anonymous, can often be brutal. There are a lot of online know-it-alls and a wide assortment of bullies who get off on blasting people. It's their only way to snatch a bit of power.

Ben felt very good about himself. He'd accomplished something that, two years earlier, he never would've imagined he would do. Or even *could* do. Remember, he wasn't even a *reader* until he was nearly 20.

But then the inevitable happened. Someone left a scathing, one-star review of his book. The words they used were cutting and cruel. Someone who didn't even know Ben, or know anything about his life story, took his two years of work and completely trashed it.

After that, while he still picked up some very nice reviews and had clearly touched some people, there were a handful of one- and two-star reviews mixed in.

Ben considered giving up writing, figuring he didn't have the talent to ever be successful.

After *one* book.

In their daily lives, Michelle and Ben might not have very much in common. Besides the generational difference, they may not share the same interests, career aspirations, or spiritual beliefs.

What they do have in common, however, is something afflicting millions upon millions of people on a daily basis, including, perhaps, you: A sensitivity to feedback that ignores what the multitudes say and hyper-focuses on the scant few that piss on their cornflakes.

I've given presentations at several writing conferences over the years, where I spoke to rooms full of authors.

Let It Be Good

More than once, I've built my presentation around something I call *Just Not Everyone*. It's a helpful reminder that applies well beyond the scope of writing. I don't see how this mindset couldn't help anyone who feels overwhelmed—perhaps even targeted—by nasty comments and toxic people.

You have hopes and dreams like everyone else, and sometimes you put yourself out there by either making a noticeable change in your life—like Michelle's fashion choice—or by attempting something outside your creative comfort zone—like Ben's brave venture into writing .

You either tiptoed into it or you dove headfirst. And, in doing so, you invited the world to comment. Because, lord knows, 21st century life has certainly trained people to comment. And then comment some more. To constantly offer an opinion, solicited or not.

When you're in the crosshairs, when you've received a snotty comment from someone who shat on your dreams, it will be hard to remember these words, but try:

There will always be people out there who will be helpful and supportive as you make your way through life.
Just Not Everyone.

When you make a decision that affects your relationship, your career, or your circle of friends, most people will be supportive and even helpful.
Just Not Everyone.

When you make a lifestyle change, whether it's to try a new hairstyle or to stop drinking, there will be people who cheer you on and have your back every step of the way.
Just Not Everyone.

What is it about us that makes those few holdouts *stand* out in our minds? Why do we allow a tiny percentage of loud people to affect us the way they do? Because, truly, we have to *allow it* for it to have any impact on us. We're practically accomplices in their assault on our self-esteem, and that sucks.

And honestly, why the hell do some people feel the need to criticize choices that are clearly important to you? Was the woman at the volleyball game really *driven* to stick that flaming hot poker right into Michelle's self-image? What compels a person to open their mouth and do that?

The troll who sits in their basement and writes searing, caustic reviews of books, restaurants, or anything—are they getting off on this? Are they even aware that the author of that book invested years of their life into their art? Do they care that a chef perhaps took a chance on creating something unique and interesting?

Of course, there are some negative reviews that are warranted. I get that. But we all know the difference between honest, constructive criticism and a shot. The volleyball mom? That was just a shot. It's not like

Let It Be Good

Michelle could run back in and have her hair reattached. (Well, there are extensions, but work with me here.)

Here's the thing: I don't want the focus right now on the people who bring us down. Let's not pay them any more attention.

I want you to focus on the power of this phrase:

Just Not Everyone.

No matter what you do, whether it's a personal change or a creative endeavor, go into it fully aware that many—and probably most—people will be happy for you. People, in general, are good.

When you get compliments for your new look, accept them graciously and bank them. When you get a five-star review for your book or for the song you recorded, or you find a glowing review online for your boutique store, revel in it. Let it drive you on to other great things. Listen to the people who encourage you.

"To Kill a Mockingbird" is widely regarded as one of the greatest novels ever written. And two percent of people give it one star in their review. Almost 95 percent give it either four or five.

If you had been Harper Lee, which number should you have focused on?

I'll bet 90 percent of Michelle's friends—her *real* friends—loved the decision she made to change something about herself.

Ben's book may not have been *"To Kill a Mockingbird"* but it was the first thing he ever wrote and published. His third, his fifth, and his tenth books will undoubtedly be better—*if* he refuses to cower in the face of a few people who know nothing of him or his dreams.

I'm rarely a rah-rah guy. It's just not in my nature.

And yet I see way too many people feel the sting of a negative review or a harsh comment and I have to speak out. It's human nature to have a certain sensitivity to these things. Hey, it hurts.

But no matter what you do, you will never, ever bat a thousand. You will never receive 100% glowing reviews.

Most people will be on your team, I promise you.

Just Not Everyone.

Chapter 7
Semi-Pro

I have a characteristic known as mixed-handedness, which is kinda fun. I write with my right hand, I shoot pool with my left. I play tennis and racquetball with my right, bowl with my left. I eat right-handed, kick left-footed. Drum right-handed, but strum a guitar with my left.

As one good friend said: *Dude, make up your mind. You're a goddamned mess.*

I played a lot of baseball as a kid, and as a left-handed pitcher I did pretty well. By age 15, I led the summer leagues in ERA. I couldn't hit for shit, but I struck out a lot of guys from the mound.

Yet in my junior year of high school, I walked away from the game because I was already working full time in radio. My trusty mitt was put on a shelf in the garage.

For several years, I questioned my decision with thoughts such as:

I should've kept playing. I was a damned good pitcher.

What if I'd played into college? Do you have any idea what a half-assed left-handed pitcher makes in the pros?

You don't even have to set the world on fire; just be left-handed and competent.

Those thoughts probably would've nagged at me forever. Until, that is, a call from a friend gave me the chance to *test* those thoughts.

This buddy, Dave, had a friend who played semi-pro baseball. These aren't the professionals you see on TV and baseball cards, but they're still good ball players. They usually keep full-time jobs and take to the diamond every summer simply because they love the game.

Dave's phone call produced a jolt of excitement. "Hey, Dom, how would you like to pitch batting practice for the semi-pro team next week?"

Are you kidding? A chance to dust off the mitt and fire strikes? Not just yes, but *hell yes*!

So a few days later, I drove to one of the more well-kept baseball fields in town and met the manager of the semi-pro team. He looked me up and down, tossed me a ball, and pointed toward the mound.

Look, this wasn't a tryout with the team. It was just one day where I participated in a practice session and lobbed pitches for the team to hit. But I was still nervous. These guys were all in their early-to-mid-twenties, same as me, and in great shape.

Let It Be Good

But come on, it's baseball. You throw the ball, they hit it, and someone else fields it. Simple.

After ten or twelve warmup pitches, the first player stepped to the plate. A big guy, at least 6-foot-4, 225 pounds. He looked so casual in the batter's box, even joking with a few teammates standing nearby.

Side note: During batting practice, the pitcher has one job. Don't get fancy, just throw the ball over the plate. It's batting practice, not pitching practice. You don't want shit in the dirt or high and outside. Throw it down the middle and let them get in their swings.

So I did. I threw several pitches that were promptly whacked, and I felt good. I still had it. I could still throw strikes. The next guy stepped in, I threw ten good pitches to him, then came the next guy. I could tell these players appreciated someone who knew how to put the ball right where they wanted it, to work on their swings without having to wade through a bunch of garbage. A few of them even tipped their cap to me as they finished.

And I started thinking. We always start thinking, right?

Maybe I really do still have it.

Maybe I could speed things up, you know, just a bit.

What if I threw a few past these guys? Throw that ol' fastball, the one that backs up on a right-handed hitter, almost like a screwball. (Remember, I'm left-handed.)

When the first guy stepped back into the box, I reared back and fired some heat. Real heat.

And he hit the shit out of it.

Well, that obviously was a fluke. I grabbed another ball, wound up, and zipped a blazing fastball just over the inside edge of the plate. Practically unhittable.

The dude hit it about 375 feet.

For the next ten minutes, I tried throwing fastballs, a few curveballs, and whatever else I had in my arsenal. And these guys never broke a sweat as they crushed almost every pitch.

After another twenty or so pitches, the manager came out, thanked me profusely, and pointed me toward the cooler of Gatorade. A couple of the players gave me high-fives for a job well done, then went out to shag fly balls.

I'd never been so dejected. I'd given everything I had, reaching down into some well of pitching prowess I'd nurtured for years as a young ballplayer, and I'd been hammered. And remember, these weren't first-class professional baseball players. They weren't even minor-league players. They were semi-pro. Not shabby, by any stretch, but not the cream of the crop. And I'd *still* been clobbered.

In the years since, I've thought about that summer day on the diamond many times. Two things stand out.

One, it was hilarious. I'd give anything to have video of the day, to see the expression on my face as I kept turning to watch the flight of a ball screaming off the bat of an otherwise-bored twenty-something. I'm sure I looked miserable.

Hey, I'm a good pitcher. I led the league in ERA and strikeouts. This can't be happening.

Oh, it happened. Over and over again.

But the second thought is powerful. So many of us carry *What-If* baggage throughout our lives. We wonder what might've been, how our world would've been different. And we carry these thoughts across multiple areas of our lives:

How would my career path have gone differently if I'd followed my passion?

What would my personal life be like if I hadn't screwed up that one relationship?

Where would I be now if I'd only listened to my gut and taken that job out of town?

You know what I'm talking about. We drive ourselves mad playing the *Sliding Doors* game, pondering missed opportunities and missed connections. It's the shitty whining we quietly do in our heads, reminiscent of "*I coulda been a contenda.*"

No, probably not. I don't subscribe to the everything-happens-for-a-reason school of thought, but I do think there are usually solid reasons why we don't make certain decisions at the time. The problem is that the *What-If* world inside our heads is always rosy—which is not realistic.

The brief set of experiences we picked up on that early path certainly played a part in shaping who we were. My teenage baseball adventures were a blast, and I learned a lot about discipline, teamwork, etc.

But there's probably no way, even with that early success, I would've excelled to where I would've made a living from it. The batting practice story backs that up.

Meanwhile, my detour into radio played out quite nicely, with a successful career that has stretched (as I write this) nearly 50 years. My love of writing turned into more than two dozen books and counting. As a professional speaker, I've entertained thousands of people in packed ballrooms. The whole notion of what could've been would only have been an anchor on my dreams, causing me to second-guess things that should never have earned a second thought.

What a blessing for me to have sweaty, tobacco-chewing young men swat my fantasies out of the park before they had a chance to fester and mushroom into some soul-draining angst.

You have dreams, you have fantasies, and those can be good—to a point.

But you also have talents. You have skills that not only make you happy, but hopefully provide you with a comfortable existence. Those talents could, if nurtured properly and enhanced through lifelong learning, explode into something way beyond those earlier dreams.

Holding on to *coulda-beens* is toxic. It not only hampers your progress, it keeps your head pointed in the wrong direction—backward, instead of forward. We only *think* we missed some tremendous opportunity because we aren't given the gift of a reality check; we base our fantasies on faint, often flimsy, evidence.

I was lucky. I got a full dose of that reality check *and* got a free Gatorade to boot.

Striking out 15-year-olds in Pony League ain't the same as trying to strike out a hot-shot 23-year-old. I wasn't good enough to be a semi-pro baseball player, it turns out. But I'm more than good enough to be a full-blown professional in three other fields.

I jettisoned my woulda/coulda/shoulda a long time ago. You should, too.

Oh, I still keep that baseball mitt around. It's a nice reminder to sit my ass down and write.

Chapter 8
Anticipation

Las Vegas is banking on the fact that I won't remember how disappointed I was the last time I visited.

Hey, I'm not dogging the place, nor am I questioning that *you* may have had the time of your life when you popped in for a few days.

For me—and I've been half-a-dozen times—Vegas is the epitome of the letdown. You're excited for the getaway and dazzled by the image of mind-blowing fun to come. You let everyone know you're going, with a subtle tone of *Don't you wish you were me?*

Then you get there, you mill around amongst the million sweaty bodies packed into a small space, you overpay for a buffet, lose a few hands of blackjack—your inevitable donation to the bottom line of the city's glittering palaces—and you feel like you're a complete and total loser because you're not having the explosively good time promised on the brochure. Or promised by your friends.

Hey, I saw *"The Hangover."* I'm supposed to be having a wild time like *that*, right?

Is there something horribly wrong with me?

No. And if you share my feelings, there's nothing wrong with you, either.

This is a classic example of the power of anticipation. Spending time in Vegas rarely lives up to the anticipation you experienced before ever boarding the plane.

And, if we're speaking the truth here, the people who insist it's always an orgasmic experience are simply trying to portray themselves as complete party animals. Trust me, they're mostly bored, too, but will never admit it. That's an entirely different article.

But it's not just Vegas.

The anticipation you have for the New Year's Eve party can almost produce a visceral tingle in your body. And yet by 10:45, you might be desperately hoping the damned clock will hurry and strike 12 so you can say your goodbyes and leave at 12:18.

By Wednesday, you're obsessively calculating just how much time has to pass before it's five o'clock Friday. The anticipation for a weekend is minor compared to the build-up of a trip, but it's still palpable.

Then the weekend comes and goes, and it was . . . okay.

I'll stop short of saying the anticipation of anything is

always better than the actual event—but I'm confident saying it's true more often than it's not.

So why is that? What is it about imagining what lies ahead that creates such a rush of feel-good chemicals?

There have been countless papers written on this, and universities have applied untold millions of grant dollars into studying it. One thing we know for sure is that the dopamine hit of anticipation actually IS bigger than the dopamine hit while we're actually doing something. Our brain knows the good stuff is in the planning.

Look at it this way: Anticipation is the Michelangelo, Donatello, and da Vinci of our subconscious. It creates a masterpiece within our mind.

For one thing, we continually rate our present state of life and look for something, *anything*, to make it better. Even if things are going swell, our natural state is to seek out better. (See the Vermont bar scene in the first chapter.)

We find ourselves thinking:

That party this weekend? I'm not currently having a good time, so THAT will provide the octane boost of fun I need.

Or:

I've had nine months of tedious work, so that upcoming vacation is guaranteed to blow the lid off the fun factor.

Our internal da Vinci, however, fails to take into account one critical factor: Wherever we're going this weekend and whatever we're doing, WE will still be the one having the experience.

It's like the old saying, 'Wherever you go, there you are.' You may be on the Vegas Strip, wearing your new shoes and sucking down a fourth cocktail, but it's the same you who was in a cubicle just 18 hours earlier. Glitzy neon signs and the sounds of strangers losing money will never change your DNA.

I spoke recently with a woman who told me she'd been absolutely giddy over the fact that she was finally retiring after working for 46 years. She even had one of those wall calendars and had eagerly X'd out the days during the last three months on the job. Can't you just see that?

During her last day on the job, her office threw a big party, everyone gave her a hug, and coworkers expressed how jealous they were.

By the end of her first month of retirement, however, she was talking to companies who were looking for help. "Retirement was the biggest letdown and biggest bore of my life," she said.

Ah, but the *anticipation* of it was better than sex. It pumped her so full of pleasure pills that there was no way in hell retirement could ever possibly live up to the hype.

Now she's looking forward to going back to work. She replaced one futuristic daydream with another.

If it sounds like I'm knocking the feeling of anticipation, far from it. I'll even admit that occasionally things *do* live up to your expectations.

Let It Be Good

But even when they don't, it's okay. While Vegas might be a major letdown, it's still a different experience. It's still a change from your normal nine-to-five routine. It's the zag to life's zig.

Not only that, but I submit that having something to look forward to—regardless of how it eventually turns out—is a remarkable tonic for the soul. Sure, the weekend may end up being filled with dreary house chores and loud neighbors, but it's a break.

And let's face it: Anticipation is *fun*. Planning a vacation will probably *always* bring more joy to your life than the trip itself, and those dopamine studies back it up.

Plus, while you're anticipating the vacation, you never think about the long lines you'll be standing in, the lost luggage, or the loud kids in the room next door.

No, your Michelangelo mind has sculpted a dreamy destination that fulfills all your wants and desires. Anticipation, if you really think about it, has served exactly the purpose it was meant to do:

It lifted your spirits and recharged your emotional battery. And that is *always* satisfying.

Chapter 9
The Cemetery

There is no train station at Chilham. Just a platform on each side of the tracks, each sporting a bench and a sign filled with information. Three cars were parked in the gravel lot outside the fence, awaiting their owners who, more than likely, had traveled to nearby Canterbury, the medieval town of Chaucer fame in southeast England.

Chilham (pronounced Chill-um) is a good fifteen-minute walk down a tree-lined country lane. Only two cars passed during my trek, perhaps tourists who'd heard about the castle in the village. They'd be returning shortly, no doubt, because the castle wasn't open to the public. A family lived there.

I trudged past a fifteenth-century pub, The Woolpack Inn, and up the street—named The Street, I kid you not; could it be any more charming?—to a modest village square. I was in search of a church, the one recommended by a train conductor during my journey to

Canterbury. I was in England alone, exploring and writing. I've taken a handful of trips like this, just getting away to unplug and to rediscover real life. You might know what I'm talking about.

I'd been the only person in the train car when the conductor approached. She was curious what this American man was doing on his own, so intent on the laptop in front of him, a beer can the only other thing on the table. We had a pleasant talk. I told her I was in search of something unique, off-the-trail, *interesting*. Ostensibly, I was scouting locations for a novel, but I was also in the mood for an introspective adventure. I wanted something you wouldn't normally find in any travel guide.

She seemed happy that someone had asked. She told me to jump off at Chilham and find the 700-year-old church. "You'll probably have it all to yourself."

And I did. There, at the top of the hill, the spire poked up from the trees, beckoning pilgrims who've been demoralized, or persecuted, or simply turned away from the castle. The grounds were deserted this late in the afternoon, save for a tired-looking elderly man who was mowing the cemetery surrounding the church.

That's one of those jobs we never even think about—but someone has to do it.

He was sweating in the hot (for England) July sun, and wore headphones I'm pretty sure were there to protect him from the mower's roar, not to rock out to Zeppelin. He'd cut a path this way and that, maneuvering through literally hundreds of headstones dotting the church grounds.

Let It Be Good

Perhaps you've seen movies with old European churches surrounded by graves, but I don't know how any of them could possibly match the solemn, mystical grace shrouding these monuments. I stood near the entrance to the grounds for a few moments, taking in the sweeping sea of stone, unsure of which direction to walk. But then I realized it didn't matter. I chose counter-clockwise and simply began.

The old man eyed me warily, but clearly was unwilling to pause in his pattern. I think he just wanted to finish and hit the pub, the one I'd passed. So I wandered to my right, toward a far corner of the grounds. I passed headstone after headstone. The first one, dated from the 1760s, immediately made me feel small, dwarfed by the weight of the centuries.

As I walked reverently around the ancient church, I saw an endless number of tombs. And I found I was becoming despondent. Not sadness because of the lost lives, but because the majority of the tombstones were unreadable. There was no record of who these people were; the inscriptions were completely worn away, the tale of each life scraped off by wind and rain and time. Many of the slabs were tilted to one side, nearly toppled; they were forlorn testaments to forgotten lives.

Their sole purpose—to account for the souls interred below—had been discharged.

At the far side of the church, I was surprised to see that, across a small lane, the cemetery continued down a hill, through a copse of trees. The old stones stretched for more than a hundred yards, along each side of paths overgrown with grass and weeds. This clearly was not the church lawn proper, and therefore not specified in the old guy's maintenance plan.

Ten or twelve feet off the path, the weeds were so high I could barely see the tops of some headstones. They were not only stripped of all information, but lost in a forgotten field, likely unseen for . . . how long?

That's when I actually felt the tears. I started weeping over people the world had misplaced. Who were they? What were their stories? Were their loved ones interred nearby, or did they die alone? How long did somebody—anybody—remember them, perhaps place flowers, maybe say a small prayer?

And at what point, I wondered, did they receive their final visit? How many generations of people had come and gone since, walking past the church without turning in to the grounds? How many others sailed past on the train, not even noticing the lonely rail platform as it whisked by their window, let alone the quiet church cemetery over the rise and beyond the trees?

The church has stood for seven centuries, and I had no idea how far back the oldest graves dated. Certainly some of them had been there from the very beginning. But hundreds were alone, adrift in the trees and the wild undergrowth, with tilted stone markers now illegible. I wept in this graveyard for people who no longer had an identity, who had no one to mourn for them or fondly remember them or their descendants. They were blank slates in a remote country field.

I'm not ashamed to admit I can get emotional. I

sometimes well up during a touching moment in a book. I've felt misty-eyed when listening to certain songs—"*Tea For One*" by Kevin Gilbert might be the saddest song ever written—and I get sentimental thinking of lost loves and lost family members.

But this was different. This was a shocking testament to how temporary it all is. Our lives are one bustling moment to another, one dot on the calendar to another. We surround ourselves with people important to us, and I suppose we want to feel like *we're* important to them, too.

It all disappears. We don't ever really stop and think about that. But it disappears. People in 1925 had their own busy lives. They had people they loved and who loved them.

They're forgotten people, too, aren't they? How many people alive today have a memory of someone from just a century ago?

The townspeople in this cemetery had been gone for 300 years. Perhaps 400. Some for 500 or more. Who remembered them?

There's an old saying, attributed to several people, so I can't list a definite origin. But the idea is that we all die twice: when we take our last breath, and the last time someone ever says our name aloud.

It's morbid to think about, perhaps. But it's also grounding, to a certain extent. We place so much importance on the mundane details of each day, and some of the most trivial elements of our lives can throw us into a frenzy.

And yet it's all so temporary. There will be a day when you not only pass from this world, but there will be a time when someone says your name aloud for the very last time.

A lesson? I don't know. Maybe to not take each day for granted? Maybe to not place such a heavy emphasis on the trivial? Maybe to appreciate the people we love just a little bit more?

Maybe to tell them?

As I left the grounds of the old church and turned back toward the rail line, I entertained a completely random thought. What if I chose this spot as my final resting place? What if I requested that my remains be buried in the farthest corner of a cemetery in the old Medieval English village of Chilham? Could I join their sacred—though neglected—patch of land? And would they want me?

For no reason at all, I like to think they'd enjoy the company of a tearful Yank.

The last person to cry over their graves.

Chapter 10
Bob Dylan Doesn't Suck

Bob Dylan ain't my thing. I don't enjoy the music or the lyrics, his unique vocal style—to put it politely—is difficult for me to listen to, and the haggard-artist look, on anyone, always struck me as contrived.

I'm well aware he has millions of adoring fans, and I give him tons of credit for not only his longevity, but for his undisputed influence on countless other artists. I'm a big John Lennon fan, and I acknowledge that Dylan was a major influence on Lennon in the mid-1960s. I believe the Beatle even referred to some of his own songs—including "*I'm a Loser*" from the *Beatles For Sale* album—as his "Dylan phase."

Side note: Legend has it that Dylan introduced the Liverpool lads to marijuana—which certainly influenced their music—although John had likely tried it already.

I never went through a Dylan phase. While the mumbling poet with the guitar and the harmonica is still lauded by many as one of America's greatest songwriters, performers, and visionaries, I shrug. To put it simply, I don't get the adulation.

Ah, but notice that not once did I say "Bob Dylan sucks."

In life, there are things we all agree should be labeled as *sucky*. Cancer sucks. Deadly hurricanes and tornadoes suck. Assholes who create and propagate computer viruses suck.

But basing a declaration of suckiness on nothing but your personal taste, *especially* when it comes to the arts, is just arrogance. I know we actually pay music and movie critics to tell us when something is godawful, but the secret truth is that nobody listens to music and movie critics. Don't tell them; they're convinced you hang on their every word.

Here's the thing, though: *I used to be that guy*.

Back in the day, if it ever came up, I would happily tell people, "Bob Dylan sucks." I'd proclaim the shittiness of The Beach Boys and Brussels sprouts, too.

Sometimes I wonder if it's an age/experience/wisdom thing. When we're young, we trot out our opinions every chance we get. When you're 18 or 20, you even think people *want* to know your opinions. *Please, oh please, tell us your take on anything and everything*. I think we honestly believe people are impressed with our every thought. (More on this in the chapter titled "Three Magic Words.")

Well, one day I finally grew up. I realized that I—like most adolescents and young adults—was actually just a bag of hot air. And practically overnight, I understood the difference between *"The Goonies sucked"* and *"That movie's not for me."*

That's the phrase I adopted: *It's not for me.*

And, surprisingly, it became freeing. It lifted a self-imposed burden I'd assigned myself—to educate the world on WHAT I THINK—and opened my eyes to the fact that no one cared. No one cared what I thought about a song or a band. We all toss out opinions, and, when you get right down to it, no one cares. People have their *own* opinions, which they value highly. Yours pretty much just serve to make them believe more strongly in their own.

So instead of "that sucks," it became "it's not for me."

It's a superior way of communicating, and I'll tell you why.

When you tell a worshipful fan of Will Ferrell that his movies suck, it practically invites argument and/or outrage. Or a punch in the face.

And why? Because you didn't insult Will Ferrel; you insulted *them*. You may as well have said, "Your taste is for shit. What's wrong with you? God, you're stupid."

When you tell that same Will Ferrell fan, "Yeah, it's just not my thing," you're practically inviting sympathy rather than anger. Now it's not that *they're* stupid, but that you're evidently not wired properly. There's something wrong with *you*, rather than with them.

And people are okay with that. Believe me, they're *totally* okay with you being the broken one.

The beauty is that both examples say exactly the same

thing: *You like this, and I don't.* One makes the other person seem to be a faulty human, while the other makes *you* the defective part.

I'll be honest, this tactic is not easy. I've done plenty of backsliding, where I sometimes catch myself mouthing off with an opinion that serves no purpose but to vent my spleen, as the old saying goes. And really, what good does it do to announce you dislike a TV show that so many other people love? Do we think it makes us seem oh-so-evolved because we *don't* watch *The Bachelor*?

I mean, we clearly ARE, but still. Why knock someone because they like something you don't? It's pointless. It's like trying to convince someone to change their political stance. Lots of pontificating with no impact.

"It's not for me" may not say it all. But it says enough. Saves a lot of time and eliminates a lot of senseless arguing—because, while you may love them, you'll never convince me that Brussels sprouts should even exist on this planet.

Nobody gets mad, we all get on with our lives, and Bob Dylan gets on with his mumbling.

Chapter 11
Paying For It

The band Stereophonics released a song in 1999 called *"I Wouldn't Believe Your Radio,"* which includes these lyrics:

> *You can have it all, if you like.*
> *And you can pay for it the rest of your life.*

The song popped up on shuffle the other day and, although I've heard it many times—and love it—this time I really focused on those two lines. In fact, I hit rewind and listened to it a couple of times, turning the lyrics over and over in my head.

Some people swim in the music of a song. I'm a word guy, and I love it when songs go way beyond "Ooh, baby, I love you." The late superstar producer Quincy Jones pointed out the big difference between artists who write *songs* versus writing just *hooks*. He believed—and I agree with him—that the modern pop music landscape is littered with hooks, but a diminishing number of real songs.

In the case of this particular Stereophonics song, I can't say what the songwriter, Kelly Jones, was thinking when he penned the words that captured my attention. But I know how I interpret them.

I look back—sometimes *way* back—at choices I've made in my life and I recognize that I'm still paying for some of them. Especially the decisions that hurt other people. I'm not sure I'll ever pay off the principal on those choices.

We don't pay for everything with money, you know. Sometimes we pay with little chunks of our soul.

Hey, my life isn't miserable. I'm quite happy. But I'm also not racing down the road of life with no feelings of guilt and regret. I've got a few. You probably do, too. Unless you're a sociopath.

I think it's important to stress that these regrets don't hobble me. They don't drive me to despair. But they're genuine feelings, nonetheless, and they have a weight to them. The choices that generated these regrets impacted me and other people, and I'd be lying if I pretended they didn't sometimes make me stop and reflect.

Many of these regrets involve intimate relationships. Some of them involve friendships, some family, some career. If every category represented a different colored pie piece in a game of Trivial Pursuit, I'd have a full set.

But to my point:

No doubt you've seen plenty of self-help memes that claim, *"You should never live a life of regrets!"* Sounds so cultured. Sounds so *evolved*. It's the kind of thing you see scattered across social media because it feels like something you *should* say, puffing out your chest and telling your digital friends, "Look at me, I've really got my life together."

Well, it's utter bullshit.

Are you telling us you clicked your heels together and magically transformed every single choice in your life into the *right* choice?

It's important—perhaps even healthy—to *embrace* your regrets, not to pretend they never happened. Sweeping stuff under the rug is cowardly. I'm firmly in the camp that our regrets are an important part of our makeup, and they deserve a place at the table.

I have many regrets I have no intention of discarding, even if I could. No matter how much pain or guilt they may still elicit, they're—in a way—gifts. If we're fortunate, these regrets help us to make better decisions later. We hope so, anyway. They're called life lessons, after all.

It's widely acknowledged that we learn much more from our mistakes than we ever do from our victories. And while that, too, sounds like a social media platitude, it happens to be one I agree with. Victories and other scattered success stories tend to flare briefly before fading. But when we stumble badly, those moments leave a psychic bruise that lingers, sometimes for years.

There must be a reason for this. Why do the wins temporarily boost us, while our losses leave a lasting stain?

I think it's because those are indeed the building

blocks for our growth. We (hopefully) learn from them. We *need* them. So to make this big production that we should always live a life of no regrets is downright foolish. Have your damned regrets. They're part of your education.

> *You can have it all, if you like.*
> *And you can pay for it the rest of your life.*

Like the song says, I'll continue paying for my bad choices for the rest of my life.

But they don't bankrupt me. They keep me grounded, they keep me introspective, and they keep me human.

Yes, I can have it all, if I like. And I'll pay for it. The good and the bad.

I mean, doesn't "all" include both?

Chapter 12
A Textured Life

I have a good friend who is all about texture. Whether it's her clothes, her home, or the design of her workspace, she is drawn to the concept of it. I'm often blind to subtle shades and layers, but I've watched her run her hand across something and murmur, "I like the texture."

Lately, I've become a budding student of texture. Rather than immediately dismissing something offhand, I'll step back and examine it for the nuances that otherwise would escape me. And, as I sat quietly the other evening in front of a fire, I realized that in order to fully enjoy *life*, it should be textured as well.

We're all guilty of falling into routines and patterns that have essentially been sanded down. We take as many shortcuts as we can, whether it's in traffic, in our jobs, or in our daily home life. We often eliminate anything that juts out in our lives at a weird angle. Weird angles create delays and detours.

And yet, it's often the detours in life that bring us discoveries.

How many times have you reached a point during your drive to work where you can't for the life of you recall anything about the previous ten minutes? I sometimes wonder if I drifted through a red light or a stop sign along the way because I'd zoned out.

But take a completely different route and you're hyper-focused on everything in your surroundings.

What about your free time? Have you become a predictable zombie, creating a perfect butt-shaped indentation on your couch?

Do you order the same meal every time at your favorite restaurant?

Do you read the exact same genre and the same authors over and over?

Or what about the time spent with your kids? Are you slowly programming their little brains to live a life without extremes? Have you indoctrinated them into the world of steady, safe routines, perhaps creating a future adult who will live life through a checklist?

I've come a long way in the past few years. I've opened myself up to activities and experiences I'd never given a chance. I've taken trips on a complete whim, including a spur-of-the-moment trip to Portugal for eight days with only a backpack.

I listen to a variety of musical artists. I'm checking off a growing number of ethnic restaurants that were on my "never ate there" list. My life has a more distinct texture.

But, like everyone else, I know I can do better. I don't

want to look back on a slick, polished, marble-smooth life. I want my life to have a wonderful extreme of textures, with more rough edges, more distinct shades and layers, and more abrupt turns.

And, like my friend, I want to feel that texture at my core.

But it's not just about our usual habits. It could also be as simple as our thought processes. Perhaps in our past we never questioned our politics, never questioned our preconceived biases toward ANYTHING (food, people, places, music).

Here, a textured life might simply be code for shaking up the status quo.

That scares many people. Hell, sometimes it scares *me*. On the radio show a few years ago, I challenged listeners on one particular day to try jumbling their morning routine. I asked them to eat something different for breakfast, to switch up the order of things they do to get ready for work—shower, brushing their teeth, etc.—and to take a completely different route to work, even if it added time to the commute.

I participated. I got up at a different time, I grabbed breakfast *before* my shower, I did none of the digital stuff I normally do in the morning, and I drove to work down roads I'd never traveled. It was a minor shakeup in a normally dull routine.

And, to tell the truth, it was refreshing. It almost seemed like an adventure, as silly as that may sound.

Naturally, most listeners did *not* take part in my little life experiment. Most said "Screw that." But many *did* try it. And the next day, I heard from several of them. Their comments included:

"That was so hard!"
"I felt off all day!"
"It was interesting, Dom, but I'll never do that again."

The responses were funny. I hadn't asked anyone to switch from using their right hand to their left hand. I hadn't suggested anyone do a completely different job from the one they were trained to do. There was no request to do anything that required additional physical exertion. These people simply tried a different breakfast or a different route to work.

So hard.
Felt off.
Never do that again.

It was total confirmation of how resistant we are to mixing up the comfortable routines we've fallen into. Or that we've become slaves to, if you want to look at it another way.

Of course, there's another possibility—and believe me, more than a few people voiced this objection. They said:

Why the hell do I need to do this? What's wrong with having a routine?

And the answer is: You don't *need* to, and there's

nothing wrong with how you're living your life. You could go the next 20 years, I suppose, without changing one damned thing about your day-to-day steps.

We certainly know people who never change a thing, like their wardrobe or their hair. They're happy in their comfort zone.

I guess my take on it is a little different. I have no reason to fight for my right to do the same thing, day in and day out. I could, like many, be content to plod along the same path.

But I'm a believer in the joy of discovery. I relish the delight of stumbling across something new. When I travel, I rarely make any plans, other than perhaps booking a hotel in advance. That week I spent in Portugal was the most disorganized, least-planned vacation I've ever taken in my life.

And I rate it as one of the greatest weeks of my life. I saw places that left me in awe, and I made friends from Europe who I'm still in touch with all these years later.

I generally read between 30 and 40 books a year. I like mysteries, thrillers, some sci-fi, but also a lot of nonfiction, mostly memoirs and biographies.

I'm not a fan of western fiction, what some call cowboy fiction. Or at least I didn't think I was. In 2013, I broke down and tried a western novel that's considered a classic: "*Lonesome Dove*" by Larry McMurtry.

And it's now on the list of my ten favorite books of all time. To give you an idea of how much I enjoyed it:

This thing is almost a thousand pages long, and at the end I was actually sad it was over. *That* is powerful.

I'd never have known that joy if I hadn't explored a genre that previously held no interest for me.

That book, like the last-minute trip to Portugal, provided beautiful texture to my life. Discovery, whether it's something we see/read, something we taste, something we hear, delivers new sensations to our brain. I'm no scientist and I have no medical data to back this up, but my anecdotal evidence is that it keeps my brain another step away from a state of atrophy. I believe our brains love texture. It's their form of exercise.

Which, if you consider that metaphor, is no different than how physical exercise helps to keep us toned and healthy. The easy, comfortable choice is to sit in that same spot on the couch. Getting up and doing something different takes an effort that part of us will fight against.

That's why the notion of switching up our routines and adding some texture to our daily lives is hard for many people. We want the easy way. We want that damned shortcut, even if it's not what's best for us.

I've made major life decisions in the last ten years or so, none of them easy—but each one acted like a pumice stone to the dead skin coating my life.

As soon as you put this book down, maybe give yourself an assignment to find one new thing to try each day. One thing. Shake up your world, even in tiny increments.

Make exploration and discovery part of your new normal.

It's possible that a life of minor adjustments on a regular basis could help to prevent major changes—the kind that happen by accident—from having the serious impact they otherwise might have.

Chapter 13
The Special Occasion

One of my favorite movies is "*Sideways.*" It's funny, it's poignant, and it has enough uncomfortable scenes to remind us how jacked up our own lives can sometimes be.

There are several memorable moments—Virginia Madsen's monologue about the life of a bottle of wine was worth the admission price alone. But one quick exchange between her character, Maya, and Miles, played brilliantly by Paul Giamatti, always stuck with me.

Miles has revealed that he has one particular bottle of wine that he's been saving for a special occasion. It's a 1961 Chateau Cheval Blanc. When Maya hears this, she tells him:

You know, the day you open a '61 Cheval Blanc—that's the special occasion.

We've built up so many myths regarding special occasions, haven't we? On the radio show, a listener told me her mother had purchased a wildly expensive set of china, but kept it all stored away in a giant hutch in the dining room. The mom claimed she'd purchased the set for special occasions.

But, as the caller pointed out, in more than 40 years, her mother *never once* broke out the china. That included the caller's wedding *and* her sister's wedding. Those occasions apparently were not special enough for Mom to soil the fancy dishes.

Another listener heard this story and called to tell us how she splurged on a dress way out of her price range, but so gorgeous that she knew it would be perfect for the special occasion that was sure to come. But it didn't seem right, she said, for the holiday party she went to, and it wasn't the right style for the weddings she attended. She said the dress hung in her closet for years, untouched, until she deemed it had fallen out of style.

There was never an occasion "worthy" of the expensive dress. It was never worn before she sold it to a consignment store. Not once.

Chances are you have a similar story, whether it's a bottle of wine, an item of clothing, or a piece of jewelry. You save it for some mystical "special occasion," even though we seem to have attached a pretty high standard in order for something to qualify as special.

Remember, for one mom, neither of her daughters' weddings met the criteria.

Let It Be Good

The first thing we could do, then, is to define the word. What makes something *special*? Is it a matter of celebration for something well done? Is it something nostalgic or personally rewarding, like weddings or an anniversary? Does a major promotion qualify?

Is it when we overcome something tragic or *potentially* tragic? If a family member beats cancer, I'm gonna go out on a limb and say that's a pretty damned special event. Break out the freakin' china, for crying out loud.

Along those lines:

I read a social media post where someone shared the news of their father's passing. They mentioned how they'd always planned on taking him on a trip to see his favorite baseball team, because, although he'd been a lifelong fan, he'd never traveled to see a game. It was one of those trips they talked about for years and years.

He died. They'll never be able to take him to a game.

I don't know if this person and their dad were waiting for some undefined special occasion to go. But they kept putting it off until the opportunity was gone forever.

This happens with many people when it comes to travel. They long to visit Europe, or South America, or even just somewhere across the country, but there's always a reason for not going: too busy, too expensive, too many other things on the calendar.

But consider this: While it's fun to think about traveling after we retire, it's also good to travel while your health and mobility are still good. Besides, once you retire, you might be on a fixed income. Travel now while you're in your earning years. Believe me, it *will* be a special occasion when you step off the plane. Stop putting it off.

There are other angles to consider. For one, could we be waiting for these special occasions because we—even subconsciously—just need something to look forward to?

As I mentioned in the chapter on anticipation, it's no secret the planning of a trip is often the most thrilling part. Your imagination goes wild thinking about how much fun it will be, what an *adventure* it will be, and often it doesn't—or can't—live up to the expectations.

So perhaps we put things off out of some unconscious fear that it won't be worth it. Maybe we don't want to waste the good feeling that accompanies whatever it is we're saving. What if the wine doesn't taste as good as we've imagined, right?

Then there's the idea that if we *do* break down and declare something a special occasion, we somehow "lose" that special thing we were saving.

I know I've been guilty of that; thinking that if I opened a bottle of Silver Oak, I wouldn't have it the next time something special happened.

Which is clearly ridiculous. There are plenty of bottles of wine, even Silver Oak, to be purchased.

We need to rewrite the narrative. The emphasis

shouldn't be on the specific reward associated with the event, but rather on the power of the event itself. Yes, we might be saving something for a special occasion, but whatever that lucky charm is, it shouldn't overpower the actual *reason* for breaking it out.

Once again, look at the mother and her beloved china. She may have focused so hard on whether or not it was the "right" time to use it that she—unintentionally, I'm sure—took some of the luster off one of the biggest days of her daughters' lives. Think of how much *more* special those dishes would've become with memories attached from those happy days.

We're almost turning this thing we're saving—wine, dress, jewelry, trip, whatever—into an emblem. We're building a mystique around this special thing in our lives, and I can't help but wonder if it's because we don't value the rest of our lives as much as we should.

Stick with me here.

Most of us see the lives of celebrities and equate those with success, with having "arrived," whatever the hell that even means. They live in gorgeous homes, they show up at all the major award shows, dressed to the nines, and they've never even had a cavity. At least, that's what we imagine.

We often feel the same way when we see the bragposts on social media. Friends show off photos of their fabulous vacation, their fabulous new home, their fabulous blah blah blah. That almost seems to be what social media has become. It's no wonder some people refer to it as BragBook.

Social media is where people go to portray themselves in the most glamorous light possible. Yeah, there are a few photos of people dressed in sweats and without makeup. But how many of those compared to the beach shots?

Between the celebs and the wanna-be celebs on Facebook and Instagram, we're made to feel like our lives are not enough. We don't have all the trinkets and all the experiences the beautiful people have. We're left with a need to define something, *anything*, as special in our own lives. Special and unique to us.

So what do we do? We grab onto something and label it as the reward for a special occasion. We hold on to it, often with no real expectation of ever deeming an occasion worthy of it, and use it to steer our ship through life.

When I'm finally good enough or successful enough, this will be my reward.

And when we don't follow through, it could be because we're just too damned hard on ourselves. We haven't—to use that term again—arrived. We haven't earned the reward.

It's nonsense. You probably have a shit-ton of things you do that deserve a reward. Hell, you could stand a reward just for rounding up your kids and getting them off to school each day. Or for dealing with an impossible boss. Or for surviving an ugly breakup, or the betrayal from a friend.

Life is rarely a cake walk. We don't need to set the bar impossibly high.

I'll dive deeper into this idea in the next chapter, "Celebrating Success."

I spent a lot of time thinking about this, and I truly believe everything we get for a special occasion should have an expiration date. No more of this "someday" bullshit. If you have an important bottle of wine, you have six months to crack it open. Whatever it is, imagine that it will dissolve into dust six months after you acquire it. It won't be there forever.

If the mom knew her oh-so-important china would crumble into little porcelain pieces, she'd use the damned plates for a pleasant Sunday afternoon roast.

If the woman who called our radio show about the dress had believed it would be a moth-damaged pile of rags in one year, she would've worn it to the freakin' grocery store. And she would've LOVED every minute of it.

Maya (the character from "*Sideways*") was on the money when she said the special occasion is when you open the wine. If your goal is a satisfied life, it should include making a conscious decision to declare more things to be special occasions.

I promise there's more wine.

Chapter 14
Celebrating Success

Now that we've covered special occasions, let's put the microscope on the idea of success.

Have you ever accomplished something that *should've* made you feel proud, and yet you just weren't able to enjoy it? It somehow wasn't good *enough*. Or, if you celebrated your success, the joy was short-lived, and you quickly fell back into a mindset of "I can do better than that."

Until I read two separate articles about the phenomenon, I thought it was simply part of my own hyper-driven personality. In reality, it's a fairly common experience.

Many of us, it seems, have succeeded—often in more than one field or in more than one segment of life—and yet we either don't see it as a success or we're too busy looking ahead to the next challenge, preparing a strategy for conquering the next mountain. We don't take the time to enjoy what we've accomplished.

The usual experts have weighed in and offered a plethora of explanations for this attitude. Some claim it's similar to the concept of *imposter syndrome*, where you feel inadequate despite success, that somehow you're not truly worthy of that success. You simply got lucky.

Some express concern that this lack of appreciation is a product of the "everyone gets a trophy" style of parenting. When a child's been raised to believe everything they're doing is the greatest feat of all time, then naturally a day will come when they see through the bullshit and realize their accomplishments aren't any better than those of anyone else.

Or they're not really accomplishments at all.

I suppose this might be true for *some* people, but it certainly doesn't apply to the rest of us. Hell, when I was young, we were lucky if we got *anything* for winning, other than a pat on the head. One of my little league baseball teams won the all-around championship and our reward was grabbing burgers and fries at a nearby truck stop. I'm not kidding.

So while this theory may have some elements of truth to it, I think the problem goes deeper than having parents who coddle.

Some go so far as to say it's a sign of depression. I'm not qualified to offer an educated response to this, except to say I've read the arguments for it and they make sense to me. It could, indeed, be a component of depression. Anyone who has fallen into this darkness recognizes the symptom, the reluctance to properly value yourself or your abilities. But, again, while it certainly can contribute to some cases, I don't think this diagnosis covers everyone.

At some point, we may have to come to grips with the fact that we might never know the exact *Why*. It's likely a case where one size does not fit all.

Speaking personally, what makes it even worse is the simple fact that I recognize this pattern of thinking in my own behavior. I can stand outside myself and see that I'm unwilling or unable to celebrate successes because I'm either too focused on the next book/radio show/*anything*, or I flat-out refuse to acknowledge that it's actually a success.

There are people close to me who express surprise or downright frustration that I shrug off any and all signs of success.

Perhaps you're the same way. You know in your heart you should be happy for an accomplishment, and yet you're reluctant to stop, relax, look back, and—I think this is key—*be kind to yourself*.

Because, really, that's what this boils down to. I was raised with a strong work ethic. I was brought up to strive. I've been competitive by nature since I can remember. And while I don't regret any of these traits—indeed, I'm grateful for them—I have to wonder if the problem is that I've never *balanced* these qualities with an equal measure of self-kindness. While I strongly believe it's the drive and competitive nature that's ultimately delivered the successes I've experienced, I'll admit I suck at celebrating them. Balance, often touted as the tonic for a happy life in general, is obviously the prescription here.

The know-it-alls say awareness is the first step toward transformation. Alcoholics begin to get help by acknowledging their disease; for that matter, *any* type of addiction is tough to overcome unless one accepts that the problem is real.

While I'm by no means implying the inability to appreciate success is as damaging as a drug or alcohol addiction, I believe it's nonetheless harmful. Our mental health is vitally important, too, and the goal of happiness and satisfaction is tough to achieve when we hobble our own progress.

Now that we've shone a light upon the issue, maybe you and I can take this knowledge and funnel it into transforming ourselves. We can shut off the mental treadmill for a few minutes, temporarily shift our minds from drive to neutral, and embrace the peace that comes from knowing—really *knowing*—that a job was well done.

Chapter 15
Passion, Ambition, Perseverance

If an inspirational quote turns out to be of dubious origin, is it any less of an inspiration?

For the past 30 years, people have attributed the following words to Albert Einstein:

*It's not that I'm so smart, it's just that
I stay with problems longer.*

Sadly, no one seems to be able to find an actual source for this brilliant comment other than a few books that now claim he said it—but the books didn't come out until at least 40 years after Einstein's death. It certainly *sounds* like something the German-born physicist and party animal might've said, but, alas, it falls into the apocryphal category.

That doesn't diminish the power of the words. Even if Einstein cribbed it from his next-door neighbor, Ernie the plumber, it's still a valid formula for potential success.

And it reminds me of an article I wrote so long ago that I don't even have a copy of it anymore, because I'm pretty sure it was stored on a floppy disk. (I wonder how many gems—from *any* writer—are lost to the mists of time simply due to the onward march of technology.)

This particular article compared three things:

Passion, ambition, and—the biggie—perseverance.

The first two are, for some people, two sides of the same coin. Let me offer some quick thoughts on those before we get to the entrée.

When it comes to our careers, passion is often misunderstood. Perhaps even misplaced. You'll hear countless speakers and authors urging you to follow your passion. I prefer to look at it another way:

> Find something you enjoy *and* you're good at, and bring your passion along for the ride.

Sure, many will disagree. They'll lecture young people to simply follow their passion and everything will be wonderful. Sounds great on a meme. But then we're left with millions of young people who can't make a living out of their passion for dancing or their passion for making social media videos and they feel cheated. "But I was *passionate* about it!"

A wise friend once counseled me to not confuse strong interest with passion. As she pointed out, you can have a strong interest in painting as a hobby or a strong interest in reading about the history of the British monarchy. But a genuine passion is something that drives you to make an actual difference, in either your world or someone else's world.

Having a strong interest in doing jigsaw puzzles is not the same thing as having a passion for becoming a nurse. One brings you joy; one changes a person's life.

Again, not everyone will agree, but I think it's a credible definition.

And, although I suppose we could also quibble over this, some so-called passions tend to have a short shelf life. We get all fired up about a particular artsy hobby and then lose interest over a few weeks or months. They're like those short crushes we have on a person until we get to know them better.

Passion can be fleeting, whether it's for a person or a career choice.

As for ambition, it's funny how it can simultaneously be revered and reviled.

Some people are ambitious as hell, and one set of people will admire their drive. Another group of people see that same ambitious person and either are suspicious of them or condemn them for their ruthless tactics. Some claim the gender of the ambitious person plays a big part in how people view them, and I believe that's often true.

Suffice to say that ambition is essentially the engine driving someone onward and upward to success.

While we likely find a passion is emotionally based,

ambition often is rooted in a logical, detail-oriented mindset geared toward achieving a specific goal. You (hopefully) have a goal in mind for your career, and the actions you take to achieve it could be defined as ambitious steps.

And while those passions can be fleeting, ambition is usually long-term, driving us onward toward the promised land.

Then we get to the third element of the equation: perseverance.

If passion is the bus we choose to get on and ambition is the engine driving that bus, perseverance is the fuel. When you run out, the engine sputters to a stop.

Perseverance is all about a mix of discipline and plain ol' resilience. I don't know how many people who *want* to run a marathon ever actually accomplish it, but statistics show fewer than 1% of people have ever finished one.

Millions of people *want* to write and publish a book, but only a small percentage ever do.

When January rolls around, millions of people want to work out and lose weight, and, well . . .

One thing these examples have in common is the consistent effort necessary to achieve success. You don't just get off the couch and run 26 miles; writing a full-length novel takes a lot of effort; and we all know the success rate of weight loss (at least prior to the new wonder drugs).

Let It Be Good

My wife knits and crochets. I watched her sit on the couch over the course of two weeks, listening to podcasts and audiobooks while crocheting a cardigan. Overall, the project took her roughly 40 hours to complete.

Now, 40 hours may not seem like an exceptionally long time in the grand scheme of things, but this was a process of mind-numbing repetition. Row after row, the front, the back, the sleeves. There's no way in hell I could do it. She, however, reached the finish line and had a gorgeous new item for her wardrobe. She persevered.

I'm an admitted over-planner. I can fill notebook after notebook with ideas and grand plans for all sorts of things, whether they're ideas for the radio show, great ideas for a future book, or even plans for personal goals. Somewhere in a plastic bin, I have a notebook with dozens of pages laying out a plan for an entire interactive website based around one young adult book series. I mean, this was a killer idea, maybe one of the best I've ever had.

I never even purchased the URL.

Hey, I can scribble notes with the best of them. You may be the same way. Then comes the actual implementation of our plans, the actions we need to take in order to turn a great idea into a great product. Or a great company.

Here's what I've noticed about perseverance. It has an intimate relationship with the other two components we've discussed: passion and ambition.

In order to persevere with something, we damned well better enjoy it or it becomes exponentially more difficult to accomplish. Just reference the weight-loss example. Ain't nobody who gets excited about that.

And we also must imbue the goal with enough ambition to see it through. If we're ambitious about fitting into our favorite pair of jeans, we're more likely to skip dessert.

In many instances, therefore, all three work together.

- Passion with ambition: We get clarity on the goal ahead, with enough excitement to motivate us.

- Ambition with perseverance: We convert our dreams into actionable steps fueled by relentless effort.

- Passion with perseverance: We stay enthusiastic about the project even when we hit the inevitable rough spots.

- All three blended together: We get a dynamic force that catapults us toward success.

Finally, there's a key ingredient to the perseverance angle, something that, if not addressed, short-circuits even the best intentions.

Burnout.

I'd written the first five books of a six-book series for young adults. I had a deadline for that sixth and final installment, and I watched the calendar pages slip by as I sat frozen. It wasn't that I didn't like the series—I *loved* the story, the characters, all of it. But I'd pumped out those first five volumes in a relatively short time span and my brain was fried.

So, even though I was under a time crunch with my publisher in New York, I set that final manuscript aside after the first 25,000 words—about a third of the target—and ignored it. For months. Tor Books needed volume six by the end of September, and in March I began writing something different. I funneled my creative energy into a project that could not have been more different.

It was like cleansing a palette. In early June, I turned back to the young adult novel—and everything just spilled out of me. Not only fresh words, but fresh ideas about how the series should end. There were plot lines that had me terrified because I hadn't known how to wrap them up, and those magically resolved, not only in a satisfying manner but in ways that were, in my opinion, terrific.

I have to wonder how the book would've turned out if I hadn't walked away. If I'd forced myself to slog through each day's writing session, I'm sure I would've finished, but I know in my soul the book wouldn't have been half as good. No way.

Perseverance is critical to success. But perseverance doesn't require 100% attention every single day. To me, perseverance is a long-term commitment that can—and maybe *should*—be sprinkled with mental health breaks.

Burnout is real. Burnout happens to everyone at some point, and often in a multitude of areas in our lives.

We can get burned out at work, at home, with certain friends, with a show we're watching on TV, with anything.

While I think the term 'life balance' is often misapplied and grossly misunderstood, there is wisdom in the concept of finding life's harmony.

A satisfied life is as much about eliminating as it is about achieving. And one thing we can eliminate is the stress brought about from burnout. No matter how passionate and ambitious we are about something, in order to persevere and reach the finish line, we have to stay *interested* in it. Perseverance for the sake of perseverance can often be a recipe for failure.

Einstein may or may not have said that his genius resulted from simply staying with a problem longer than the average scientist would, toiling away after others might've given up.

He clearly was passionate about his scientific ideas, he was determined to find answers to questions, and he stayed up late working on the solutions. He persevered.

Here's hoping you fall in love with an idea and see it all the way through.

Chapter 16
Discerning

Let me pose two questions to kick off this chapter.

Does a product need to be good in order to rack up large sales?

And conversely, if something sells like crazy, does that mean it must be good?

A few years ago, a coworker and I disagreed on the merits of a particular hit song. He pointed out that this piece of music had racked up over two *billion* views on YouTube. In his mind, this meant it automatically was an excellent song. I think he even said, "You don't get two billion views if it's not good."

But is that right? We base our quality judgment on a YouTube scorecard?

Social media success feeds on itself. When a certain number of people view something on YouTube, that triggers an algorithm to force-feed it to millions of additional viewers. From there, the machine will pump it out to even more eyeballs.

My wife has nearly 200,000 followers on a social media account where she educates people about growing and foraging for mushrooms. She knows if one of her videos hits a certain level of popularity, the platform will push it out to the universe. That's why she has videos with 1,000 views, while others have millions of views.

The social media platforms have learned very well how to make something viral in order to capitalize on advertising dollars. Should we anoint something as "good" when the robots have simply spoon-fed it to millions—or sometimes billions—of people?

That means the algorithm is, in a way, deciding what constitutes *quality*. And millions of people, like my old coworker, blindly accept this analysis: *Hey, a lot of people listened to it. Therefore, it must be great.*

The character Niles on the TV show *"Frasier"* once uttered this line: "Popularity is the hallmark of mediocrity."

Was he wrong?

If a restaurant brought out a plate of Kraft Mac N Cheese, then why go? Stay home and make it. We go to—and we enjoy—nice restaurants because the chef has created something we *might* be able to duplicate . . . but probably not. He/She has years of training and hands-on experience. I'm good in the kitchen, but not like these guys.

If all it took was finishing a paint-by-numbers scene of dogs playing poker to wind up in the Louvre, then we wouldn't be impressed, right? Monet, Matisse, and

Let It Be Good

Picasso have works worth millions because you and I probably couldn't do it.

We each have a quality barometer in our heads that identifies something as either good, bad, or so-so. For me, one prerequisite is simply:

Could I do it?

Let me explain and then see if you agree.

I never properly learned to play an instrument. For a few years as a kid, I banged around on a set of drums in the basement, but I never became proficient. In sixth grade, I tried out for the school band, but the teacher chastised me for holding the drumsticks wrong and pointed to the door.

I didn't know there was a "wrong" way to hold them. I simply gripped them the way my drumming idol, Ringo Starr, did it. Apparently, the Beatle would also have been denied entry to the *prestigious*—yes, that is sarcasm—River Road Junior High band.

As an adult, I got the itch to play the bass guitar. (I'm obviously a rhythm section guy.) So I found a used, left-handed bass and a small amp for $150 and watched YouTube videos on how to play the bass.

It didn't take. The truth is, I didn't invest the proper amount of time to really learn. Or maybe I was simply too old to learn. I recently read an article that said the optimal time to learn anything is when you're 26. That could be true, it could be total garbage. But if it's accurate, I'd missed my window with the bass by about 20 years.

I ended up selling the damned thing in a garage sale, along with the amp, for $100. My failed two-year experiment cost me fifty bucks.

Clearly, I was not born to be a musician. My skills lay elsewhere.

I tell these stories about the drums and the bass to emphasize that I really don't have the proper *curriculum vitae* to critique a professional musician's work. At least, in the minds of some people. If you haven't done it, they'll say, you can't criticize it.

That's bunk, isn't it? Movie critics aren't filmmakers, and yet they happily spew opinions for all to see and hear. Restaurant critics aren't former chefs. Fashion critics have usually never even sewn on a button. So why can't you or I offer an opinion on songs and albums?

Anyway, here's what I know:

When I hear certain songs, I'm pretty sure I could spend ten minutes with GarageBand on my Mac and crank out something similar.

Mind you, this is not a rant from an old guy who hates new music. I'm an old guy who *loves* new music—just not uninspired pablum that required minimal work. When I listen to Spoon's *Gimme Fiction*, or Fleetwood Mac's *Rumours*, or The Dandy Warhols' *Thirteen Tales From Urban Bohemia,* or Beck's *Guero,* I hear real musicians writing well-crafted songs, displaying talent they spent years refining.

I couldn't do that. I could never produce really good music. I tried learning, but . . . didn't.

So when I hear something that doesn't—in my mind, anyway—require the hundreds or thousands of hours that real musicians invested in their art, I'm more apt to shrug. And I'll often think, *I could've done THAT*. Just hit a few computer keystrokes and pump out some repetitive sounds and finger snaps. Don't forget those ever-present finger snaps.

I hear some pop songs and honestly think, *Dang, I could knock that out in an afternoon*.

You might respond with, "Oh yeah, big talker? Then try it!"

The point is, I *think* I could, and that's enough; they haven't earned my respect.

But could I sit down and pound out "*Sgt. Pepper*", or "*London Calling*", or "*Nevermind*"? Nope. Not a freakin' chance.

I feel the same way about other artistic endeavors. I may be a writer, but sometimes I finish reading a book and say, "Wow, I could never do that."

With Harper Lee's "*To Kill a Mockingbird*", or books by Michael Chabon or Neil Gaiman, for instance, I recognize they spent years learning their craft, writing millions of words before they "arrived." You can't just crank it out at your kitchen table in one day.

Side note: Yes, with artificial intelligence, you now *can* crank it out—but it wouldn't really be yours, so we'll shelve that thought for now. Let's stay on point.

There's some incredible talent writing young adult books today, either in composing beautiful prose or in mastering the telling of a tale, sometimes both. I believe J. K. Rowling created real magic with her storytelling. I think Louis Sachar's *"Holes"* is fantastic, and John Green's *"The Fault in our Stars"* is generational.

On the other side of the coin, I believe other mega-hyped young adult books have sold a bazillion copies with writing that's pure crapola. Hell, some of the more popular teen books and movies read as if they were written BY a thirteen-year-old girl instead of FOR a thirteen-year-old girl. Apologies to thirteen-year-old girls.

I bow down in awe to the writers who exhibit the kind of wordplay that's truly a gift. The problem is marketing and influencers can make bad writing into a hit.

Which leads to that first question at the beginning of the chapter: Yes, they sell a ton—but does that make them *good*?

I know some people are afraid to be discerning, fearing they'll be labeled a snob. That's nonsense. Hold artists to a higher standard. Force musicians and authors and chefs to raise the bar, to constantly improve. The talented ones will do it, trust me.

But if they know they can fling dog poop on a plate

and you'll happily lap it up, then what would possibly motivate them to create a masterpiece?

Yes, I'm clearly an advocate of letting something be good. We shouldn't always try to squeeze more *goodness* out of something.

But first, it has to reach the level of good.

I'm not disparaging McDonald's hamburgers; you may love them, and that's fine. But nobody, not even the top brass at the Golden Arches, would ever label their burgers as fine cuisine. And yet, if you go by nothing but sales figures, as that former coworker believed, they would have to be considered the finest quality hamburgers in history.

Do you see how the quality/quantity equation doesn't always balance?

I debated including this chapter in the book for two reasons.

One: It could be construed as contrary to the premise of the theme. *We're supposed to just let things be good, Dom. What is this?*

I *do* want to let most good things bask in their goodness. But I worry we've let our standards dip to the point where anything can be labeled *amazing*. When everything is amazing, nothing is amazing.

Two: It's too easy for people to refuse to be discerning because they think it makes them a snob, an elitist, or whatever pejorative you want to use.

Come on. It's in our best interests to insist on quality. Hold out for the exceptional and you'll get less garbage.

Consider Hollywood. They continue to release sequel after sequel after sequel, so that now it's almost laughable—and yet they won't stop. Why not? Because consumers give them a pass and continue to buy tickets. People even grumble that almost every movie is a sequel/prequel/spinoff while they line up to buy tickets.

If everyone refused to see the 8th installment in a lame movie series, there wouldn't be a 9th. The movie studios care about NOTHING except the bottom line.

Pop music has slipped into something you could almost call the doldrums. There are fewer and fewer artists making interesting albums. They know the simple, tried-and-true hooks will work, will sell, and they can knock out an album in just a couple weeks.

And people refuse to hold them to higher standards. So that's pretty much all you'll get.

I propose that people are now fearful of being discerning. The preposterous overuse of the term *hater* has many tiptoeing around anything that might seem the least bit critical. It implies that holding someone or something to a higher standard is harsh or disrespectful.

But the Cambridge Dictionary defines discerning as "showing good judgment, especially about style and quality."

And that's a *bad* thing?

Think of the areas of your life where you could—or should—be discerning.

Let It Be Good

The people you do business with.
The social media content you engage with.
The people you have intimate relationships with.

Each of these—and many more—not only can affect how successful you become in life, but ultimately how happy you are with your life. And that combination of success and happiness plays an immense role in building a *satisfied* life.

No, we don't need perfection. But there's nothing wrong with holding out for good. And if you don't get it where you're looking, look somewhere else, whether it's music, film, food . . . or people.

Chapter 17
Three Magic Words

Poets, novelists, theologians, filmmakers, and countless social media memes have drilled it into our heads that the three most important words in the English language are:

I love you.

Really? *Those* are the three most important words? I agree they can open your heart, they can help you form a bond with someone, and they certainly sell a lot of greeting cards.

But while I've definitely said *I love you* to the people I'm closest with, I've also expressed it to pets. And while I may not have said the words aloud, the same sentiment has popped into my head when presented with a pepperoni pizza. And if you've never fallen in love with an oatmeal-chocolate chip cookie, then you haven't experienced Gretchen's baking.

So yes, those are three powerful words. But I nominate another three-word phrase as the most magical, and one of the keys to a satisfied life:

I don't know.

We're a prideful species. We hate to admit we don't know things—which is ridiculous. People even feel embarrassed when they're confronted by something about which they're ignorant.

Ignorance is an often misunderstood word. Many people equate it with stupidity, and that's not the case. Ignorance is simply a lack of knowledge or awareness of something.

There's a guy who comes to the house a couple times a month to treat my lawn. He'll tell me about soil science and disease control specifications of various turf applications, and I couldn't be more ignorant. I nod, I pay him, and I go back inside my house. Am I stupid because I don't have the specific knowledge he has? No. He was trained with this information. That's why he has that job and why I host a morning radio show.

We're probably not that far away from having chips placed inside our heads, then plugging into a database and simply downloading anything we want to know straight into our brains. In fact, we're probably a lot closer than you think. We've already begun implanting chips for other reasons; this would just be the next logical step.

Let It Be Good

Until that happens, we *can't* know everything. So why do we feel so embarrassed about it?

In his fascinating memoir called "*Sonny Boy*", Al Pacino says:

> *Who wants to wallow in the pretense*
> *of knowing everything?*

Yeah, it's exhausting having to put on a show, acting as if you're omniscient. And when it comes to living a satisfied life, there are things that actually make ignorance a gift.

One: It actually opens the door to learning.

When we pretend to know stuff, we close the door to actually *educating* ourselves about it. I'll never understand everything my lawn expert is doing out there, but when I honestly tell him, "Dude, I have no idea what you're talking about," he smiles and teaches me a little bit. I don't absorb all his know-how, but I learn enough to make some better decisions moving forward.

It's not like I came out of the womb knowing how important the words *I don't know* could be. Like many young people—and perhaps most men—I would stubbornly act like I knew everything. It's almost a hallmark of young adults; we're desperate to impress, and one way to do that is to seem all-knowing. I suppose it's a way of trying to earn acceptance within the tribe.

It's a joke. We basically don't know shit, but our ego won't allow us to say, "I don't know." My step-daughter dated a young man, about 20 years old, who came to a holiday dinner and proceeded to have a comment about *every single topic* that was brought up. You could tell with almost every utterance that he was completely talking out of his ass and didn't know the first thing about most of the topics.

He was so eager to show off how brilliant he was that he could not have appeared more idiotic. I almost felt sorry for the guy. I wanted to take him aside to coach him:

"Dude, you don't have to act like you know everything. YOU'RE TWENTY. Just sit back and absorb."

You probably know the old saying: *Better to remain silent and be thought a fool than to speak and remove all doubt.* That's often attributed to Abraham Lincoln, and it certainly sounds like one of his pearls of wisdom, but the actual origin is unknown.

The point is, it's almost in our genes to come across like we know stuff. The truth is, we're not fooling anyone.

It's one benefit of aging: We lose that adolescent trait of craving acceptance, and instead grow to realize it just doesn't matter. A young man at 20 wants it; an older man of 50 couldn't care less. And not caring about *that* is freeing.

It's also why older people seem to have no filter when they speak. If you're of a certain age, you know how fantastic that is.

By saying *I don't know*, you allow yourself to learn. That's valuable.

Let It Be Good

The second thing makes it a gift, too—but not for you.

When you tell someone *I don't know*, you're elevating them in that moment. You're graciously ceding the intellectual high ground to them. That's a nice thing to do.

There are times I can tell someone is truly proud of the tidbit they know, and I'll *pretend* to not know it, just to let them shine. Do that once and see how warm it makes you feel. It doesn't hurt anyone. You're not really lying; you're just letting them feel good about what they know.

I listen to a lot of podcasts, and I also coach podcasters. One thing I hear far too often when two people are talking on a podcast is the embarrassing struggle between them to see who's the first to share some piece of information. They'll often interrupt each other, just to show off that I KNOW THAT, TOO!

No one is impressed. I'm *more* impressed if you sit back and let the person relate the information.

When you say *I don't know*, you're providing a gift to the person who *does* know. It's a measure of kindness.

One last thought about the three magic words:

I subscribe to the belief that it's better to know a little about a lot of things than to be some know-it-all in only one subject. Some would call it being well-rounded. I don't know everything about the Civil War, but I know a few important items and dates. I don't know everything about European geography, but I have more than a passing knowledge. I don't know everything about the solar system, but I know a good deal. I can carry on conversations about any of these.

To me, it's not unlike the evolution of how young people pursue hobbies and interests.

When I was a kid, we played lots of sports. We played baseball, football, basketball, and anything else that cropped up. My buddies and I picked up tennis rackets and gave it a go. We messed around with the various track events, from the hurdles to the high jump to the long jump. None of us went on to become pros, but we got pretty damned good in a few of them, and could hold our own in *any* of them.

We played chess, we played pool and air hockey, we built treehouses, we climbed trees, we built our own go-carts. We were like Renaissance kids.

Today, a huge percentage of kids are funneled into one sport from a young age, or one hobby, or one intellectual pursuit—and their entire lives are devoted to that one thing. They go to practice before school, again after school, and all of their summer camps are devoted to that one thing. Will their adult lives be based on that? Probably not. And I feel bad for them. I feel like they're missing so many of the *flavors* of childhood.

I look at knowledge the same way. I love to hear about young people who are dabbling in a variety of topics and fields. It breaks my heart for kids to take "assessment tests" in middle school and to be told they're best-suited for this or for that.

Are we losing our minds? You would really take the

precious blank slate that makes up a 13-year-old and insist they should focus on *this one thing*?

That's nuts. Let their minds drift from idea to idea, from hobby to hobby, from book to book. Trust me, they'll usually settle on the thing they're meant to pursue. And if they don't at first, they can always change tracks.

I swear it's good for the brain. Otherwise, it's like going to a gym and doing nothing but biceps exercises. Ridiculous, right? And yet that's what we're doing with our brains, and with the brains of our students.

A truly satisfied life is one where we never stop learning. Where we embrace our ignorance and almost celebrate it, because it offers us another opportunity to learn.

Where we no longer are afraid to say *I don't know*.

Chapter 18
The Goldilocks Choice

A famous rock star, through a haze of cigarette smoke and a table covered with empty bottles, once claimed that a 32-track audio recording was ridiculous.

Why? Because, he said, while a producer might love the power of orchestrating so many inputs and manipulating the wide spectrum of sound, the average person can't distinguish more than eight tracks. We like to think we have finely tuned ears, but we really don't.

And are all those tracks even necessary? Many critics argue that the album *"Sgt. Pepper's Lonely Hearts Club Band"* is the greatest rock record ever made.

The Beatles recorded it using a four-track machine.

Side note: That album plays a big part in the upcoming chapter called "The Gift."

The rock star's casual observation holds another simple truth:

We *think* we want a lot of choices in our life, but

deep down, that's bull. A bushel of choices only creates noise and anxiety.

It starts early in life, too. We plead for the 64-count box of crayons, certain we need all of them. Then we wind up using our favorite six. Desert Sand and Magic Mint come out maybe once or twice, certainly never enough to require the fancy built-in sharpener in the back.

It accelerates from there, until one day you're standing in the cereal aisle, dumbfounded, trying to differentiate between a dozen distinct varieties of Special K. Can they *all* be Special?

Ever been in the mood for a movie and then fallen into a scrolling coma on your couch, unable to decide from the endless titles rolling past your overwhelmed eyes?

Choice in reasonable doses is good, and I doubt anyone would voluntarily ask for fewer options. That's because we're brainwashed into believing the pallet with hundreds of choices is a gift from the gods, like they're doing us a big favor.

But we all know more is rarely better. Fifty shades of crap is still crap, no matter how they alter the packaging.

Business owners love for you to fall for the misguided belief that their dazzling display of options makes them look like they care about us.

That's backwards. They're making us work too hard.

It's easy to choose between two or three things and feel confident in your selection. Your brain isn't taxed and you feel reasonably capable of selecting the best out of three. At least the odds are good.

But when there are 20 options staring you in the face, you'll never believe your choice is based on anything logical or concrete. It simply becomes a random selection so you can just be done with it.

There's also the classic issue of analysis paralysis. The process of choosing becomes so overwhelming that you make no decision at all. I mean, have you seen the menu at The Cheesecake Factory?

It actually goes beyond our brain's natural capacity for problem solving. A restaurant consultant once wrote that seven items per category was the *maximum* for ordering efficiency. Appetizers? Offer only four or five. Entrees? Give the customer no more than seven. Desserts? Three or four is optimal.

Sure, it sounds contrary to what we normally find. But the experts know what they're talking about. Any more than seven and the customer merely freaks out and orders the same thing she always does.

Ah, you're nodding. You order the same thing over and over again, too, right?

I have fond memories of a popular dive bar in Sedalia, Colorado that totally understands this model. Their menu has a total of four items:

- Hamburger
- Double-Meat Hamburger
- Cheeseburger
- Double-Meat Cheeseburger.

That's it. Pick one and sit down. Oh, and they don't clutter things in the kitchen with fries, either. No, your choices for a side consist of a bag of chips or nothing.

The place is always packed.

Now, I'm not saying its popularity is entirely based on the stress-free menu, but it probably doesn't hurt. And honestly, in all the years I've known about the place, I've yet to hear of anyone muttering a complaint about the menu. If anything, it has added to the lore of the place.

What we secretly long for is the Goldilocks solution, the one that's "just right." You can sum it up like this:

Please let us choose between only three. That way I can choose the one in the middle.

We can easily handle three. There's something symmetrical about it, I suppose. In fact, a few companies have learned a little trick.

Give the consumer three size options and that consumer will pick medium. Almost every flippin' time. Well, besides a certain coffee joint; they've trained people to go big.

But most places eliminate the possibility of you ordering a small by offering a medium and a large, thereby increasing their profits.

The medium is the Goldilocks, and it makes most of us really, really happy.

Online businesses, especially those offering subscription models, do it all the time. There's an entry level, which they make clear is for losers. There's the big honkin' mega-deal, which seems way too extravagant for our needs.

Then they highlight the choice in the middle, and usually have it marked with something along the lines of "Most Popular" in bold type. They know that's the one most people will select. We don't want to feel cheap, and we don't want to overspend—but that one in the middle sounds lovely, doesn't it?

They planned on you getting that one from the moment you clicked on the link.

And, just so you know, they jacked up the price of the gaudy choice on the right—I mean *considerably* jacked it up—so they could raise the price of the one in the middle and you'd still feel like you got a bargain.

This is not just idle chatter. It's a strategy taught by some of the best marketing geniuses in the world.

We seem to find personal satisfaction in the Goldilocks choice. I sometimes wonder if, visually at least, it provides us with comfort because it's bracketed. We don't feel extreme in our choice; we didn't go too low and we didn't get suckered into going too high.

Oh, we were suckered, all right.

But willingly.

The Goldilocks choice even shows up in our personal choices. There are hilarious memes about people—both men and women—who tolerate a certain amount of craziness or bad behavior because the other person is hot.

As we mature, however, we realize the comfort zone is often not to be found with the hottest mate—the legendary 9.9, if you will. (I don't believe in 10s, remember?) We learn that a stable, honest, and reliable 6 or 7 is far superior when it comes to our mental health.

Are there exceptions? Of course. There are probably many 9.9s walking around who are wonderful people. But playing the law of averages, I'm confident most people have nightmare stories about the super-hot man or drop-dead-gorgeous woman they once dated before coming to their senses.

There's also the problematic issue of "checking all the boxes." Some single people have created a long list of qualities a potential mate must exhibit: a certain height, a certain body style, with interests and hobbies that align with their own. They must own a home, or drive a nice car, or have a certain credit score.

It's funny that the longer someone is single, the shorter that list becomes. We learn that too many items on the "must have" list don't seem as important anymore. Pretty soon we learn to look for someone who's kind, reliable, and fun to be around.

It takes a while, but there comes a time when we grudgingly—with a laugh and a shrug—admit WE'RE not a 9.9 either.

Hey, if you're happily single, cheers to you. I get it. I was single for many years, and very happy.

With careers, we sometimes choose between a job we absolutely adore or a job that pays more. The problem is the well-paying job can also steal our soul. It's like making that proverbial deal with the devil.

So millions of people learned to find the Goldilocks job. It pays just enough without consuming us. Just ask former attorneys who are now teaching, or investment managers who now work for a non-profit. They've found that comfortable middle ground.

You may be teetering on the edge of a tough decision in your professional life. You love the money you're making, but not the *person* you're becoming. It's hard to walk away from a substantial paycheck, that's for sure.

But how happy are you? Is it time to find your Goldilocks?

The rock star was right. Thirty-two tracks aren't necessary to make great music. We don't need, nor really want, 25 different kinds of Oreos. We're pretty damned content with the originals.

Three soup choices on the menu are plenty. Honestly, we'd probably be satisfied with two, as long as one of them is French onion or tomato bisque.

And, ultimately, with almost any decision, we're happier to just flip a coin. Nobody was ever paralyzed having to choose between heads and tails.

We call it, we watch the result, and we get on with our life.

Chapter 19
Halfway There

There are road trip people, and there are people who would rather have a flaming thimble of Tabasco thrown into their eyes.

I'm in the first group.

I was raised on road trips, cumulatively spending hundreds of hours in the back seat with my sister, Donna, as our dad drove us up and down interstate highways and two-lane back roads. We logged more than a thousand miles of unpaved gravel on the ALCAN highway to Alaska, and we did it roundtrip. *Twice*.

Those experiences early in life either condition you to be a road-tripper, or they traumatize you to the point where you can't stand to be in a car for more than an hour at a time.

For me, you load up with your favorite car snacks— I'm a freak for trail mix and peanut butter M&Ms—and you hit the road.

But there's something I've discovered as I've logged

my own thousands of miles behind the wheel. Planning your trip and then driving there each deliver a huge hit of dopamine. There's almost no greater excitement than pulling out of the driveway as you head off on a grand touring adventure.

Coming back? Well, it's not nearly as fun. You've been in the car for hours, the cooler now has baggies of snacks floating in melted ice water, you've exhausted yourself at your vacation destination, and now you're faced with hundreds of miles, if not a thousand or more, until you're home. And going back to work.

In early 2024, I took a solo road trip to witness the total solar eclipse that cut a path across the U.S. I ended up as far north in Vermont as you can get before needing a passport. Seriously, I took a photo of a sign that said: *Canada, 1 mile.*

The drive *to* the eclipse was like a high. When it was over, and I fell into the biggest traffic jam of my entire life —I think everyone in New England went to Vermont— it was a dreary, frustrating low.

At least I was able to finish two complete audiobooks during my solo time in the car.

So the first half of your road trip vacation is a blast, and the last half . . . not so much.

I suggest the ideal recipe for a vacation might be:

Rent a car.
Do the outbound leg of your road trip.
Have a ball at your destination.
Then FLY home.

Let It Be Good

You'd feel the rush of planning and driving *toward* the fun, but then the return would be quick and painless.

I've noticed the first half of most things can be noticeably better than the second half. To wit:

I watched my wife, Gretchen, as she toiled away, knitting a sweater. When I looked over and asked to see her progress, she held it up and announced she was on "Sleeve Island."

That meant nothing to me. She explained that the term, used by countless knitters, describes the joy of finishing the first sleeve of a shirt or sweater before realizing you have to do it all over again for the second arm.

Sleeve Island.

Gretchen says many people in this position find another knitter in a similar spot, and they'll actually swap sweaters. The other person will knit YOUR second sleeve while you knit theirs. That way, you still feel excitement over a "new" project, but really what you're doing is rowing somebody off Sleeve Island while they do the same for you.

It's funny how we play these mind games.

Writers talk about something called "Starting Energy."

You get an adrenaline rush beginning a new writing project, whether it's a book or a screenplay or a long article. You fly through the first 5,000 to 10,000 words of your novel, the story springing from your brain to your fingertips as quickly as you can type it.

Then you hit what some call the Soggy Middle, others the Sagging Middle. More candid writers come right out and say it's the Shitty Middle. The adrenaline has worn off and the story has stalled. You're no longer fueled by enthusiasm to sit down and crank out another 1,000 or 2,000 words to make the day feel like a success.

There are some writers who plot and plan the entire book before they write a single word, hoping to ease this mid-book lull, and then others who just wing it the whole way through. There are no right or wrong methods; you do what works best for you.

The point is: Coming up with the idea for a book is easy, and writing the first half is often a breeze. It's the "driving it home" portion that becomes challenging.

Naturally, because of how my mind works, I began extrapolating this notion of First Half/Second Half to see if it pertains to other areas of our lives.

And of course it does.

Careers

I've been working for 47 years, and in that time I've had exactly four job interviews. I must've bombed the first one, at age 15, because Piggly Wiggly didn't hire me. My dream of bagging groceries crashed and burned.

The next three interviews were at radio stations, in

Let It Be Good

1977, 1986, and 1993. I guess I learned how to say the right things, or how to really fool people, because those all worked out and turned into the only three jobs—other than writing—I've had in my life.

Now think of *your* job interviews. You may not have been over the moon about all of them, but you probably went into each of them with high hopes and a positive attitude.

Likewise, our first days or weeks on a job are generally exciting. Sure, plenty of people continue to love their job, but others reach a point where it's a slog. I've loved some jobs while not being crazy about the people I worked with. We often can tolerate them for a certain amount of time before it makes the job itself unattractive.

Or perhaps your skills increase to where you need more of a challenge.

Or perhaps the company isn't adopting the skills necessary to compete, and it leaves you frustrated.

Or . . . fill in the blank.

I know there's a school of thought that you should change jobs and/or careers every few years in order to accelerate your progress up the fabled ladder. Hey, that's a decision you need to make for yourself. I'd simply warn you to be careful of littering your resume with a trail of jobs lasting just a year or two; that's often a red flag that you're either difficult or someone who merely wants to use a job as a springboard. That topic is a book unto itself.

What I'm suggesting is that you perform an honest

audit of the situation before you bail. You might just need a vacation. And I'm not kidding.

But I'm willing to bet that when you finally decide to leave, you'll be able to look back and see there was a point about halfway into the job when you first got the wandering eye.

Relationships

It's funny how our career relationships and our personal relationships tend to run in parallel. For many people, if not most—including me—both are important to our happiness.

And they both have lifecycles. Some people meet the love of their life in their teens, never date another person, get married, spend their entire lives together, and die holding hands. Or something like that.

That's beautiful. It's also rare. But whenever I talk on the radio show about relationships, I'm guaranteed to hear from one or two people who have this exact story. Well, they haven't got to the dying-holding-hands part yet, but they're on that trajectory. And they always speak as if EVERYONE has—or should've had—this same experience, as if the rest of us are big weirdos because we didn't meet our life partner when we were 15 years old.

Obviously, most people go through a handful of relationships before meeting "the one." Sometimes these early pairings are intense, and might even progress all the way to marriage. But these practice partnerships break down, either because of the other person's shortcomings, or yours. Or many times there's nothing wrong with either person; you're just not "right" together. I touched on this briefly in the chapter titled "The Wrong Path."

When I look back at some people I dated in my single years, I can admit I knew halfway through that it would not work out. But I did what many people do—probably what *you've* done—I hung in there, thinking it could work out.

It couldn't. It didn't.

The second half of your failed relationship is where you accumulate evidence to back up your initial warning signals that it wasn't going to work. The first half of your time together was wonderful. The second half was not so good, and probably involved an exit strategy you worked out in your mind.

Of all the chapters in this book, this one took the longest to write. It also contains the most deleted material, culled from the original manuscript and stored in a separate file. Honestly, I took out enough to populate an entire new chapter.

Why? Because my original vision for "Let It Be Good" was a hopeful, uplifting look at the elements that contribute to a satisfied life. And so much of *this* chapter could be seen as a downer.

Gretchen saw an early draft and her response was: "You're saying the second half of everything in our lives is shitty? That's depressing."

First of all, I hope I'm not giving the impression that

the second half of *everything* is, as she said, shitty. I would say it's just often not as shiny. The second half of a road trip may not be as good as the first half, but it's still a vacation. Your last few months at a particular job may not provide the dopamine boost you got on Day One, but the job still provides an income, hopefully insurance coverage, and allows you to hone your skills.

And who says these realizations have to be depressing? Why can't they be constructive? This might simply be one of those cases where it's all about perspective.

Let's use every example I listed above:

The road trip:
You can either try the elaborate solution I suggested, combining both driving and flying. Or, if you drive back, you could build in an extra day and take a different route, providing you with an entirely new experience—at least visually. Some of my all-time favorite vacation moments came when I deviated from "the plan."

Gretchen's "Sleeve Island" dilemma and solution:
She meets other people who share her passion. She also gets a free tutorial by witnessing first-hand someone else's techniques and style.

A writer's Soggy Middle problem:
There's an opportunity to briefly work on something

else. It's a reset button for a writer's brain, and it leads to some unexpected gems. When I got stuck on one of my Eric Swan novels, I took time out and wrote a Swan short story, set at Christmas. It became one of my favorite stories, and I knocked it out in less than a week. A total bonus. And, since I offer it free every Christmas, other people receive a gift, too.

The career crisis:

This one should be obvious. It provides you the nudge you may have been waiting for to either jump to another job that feeds your soul, or to finally take that leap and start your own business.

The poet William Butler Yeats said: "Do not wait to strike till the iron is hot; but make it hot by striking."

There's a long list of people who will testify that dream jobs are often born out of frustration. The second half of your career could be viewed not only as an exit, but as an on-ramp.

And then, with personal relationships, I have so much to say. But let me condense it down to something simple.

It took me years to realize that most of us make the mistake of looking at our own relationships through another person's lens. THEY have a definition of a good relationship, THEY tell you what's important in a relationship, and THEY create the template for what works in THEIR relationship.

Many people suffer from comparison-itis. It might be their parents' beautiful relationship, or a sibling's successful 30-year marriage. Or the storybook romance experienced by a good friend.

They are not you. If their definition and their framework works for them, hallelujah. But comparing your life to someone else's life is a big mistake, with relationships or anything else.

Remember, you're only seeing snapshots of another person's life. They might put on a good show in public, but then suffer in silence when they're home. And for all you know, they're envious of *your* life.

Relationships are like the swells of the ocean; you go through high points, then dip down into a trough. We ride those ups and downs because that's the natural cycle of life. But you know when something is not right and not just a trough. If you're honest about it and assess it based on what's true and real—and not just a bad day— you'll be able to navigate through.

There's either a wonderful relationship waiting on the other side, or there's a single existence that will also provide you with a happy life. Staying in a bad relationship is not superior to a healthy, satisfied single life.

The second half of a bad relationship is valuable because it teaches you about what you DON'T want.

And that's not depressing. That's refreshing.

Chapter 20
The Gift

I was raised by a strict military man. He was a first sergeant in the Air Force, truly a tough guy. Not that he didn't have a heart. He loved his wife and kids, but he definitely was not what came to be known as the "sensitive new-age guy."

And that meant he had no time for long-haired hippies or rock-n-roll. Like many from his generation, rock music was just noise. I seem to recall John Lennon referencing the critics who called his art "electronic noise." That summed up my dad's feelings.

It didn't help that so many rock stars back in the day were drug-addled much of the time. So now you've got the combination of long hair, drugs, and rock music. I doubt many first sergeants in the 1960s or 1970s thought much of that.

The problem was, an older sister had exposed me to a lot of that music. Debra introduced me to several rock-n-roll hits from the 1960s. And after she graduated and moved away, I somehow inherited her vast collection of 45 RPM singles, which included classics from the Kinks, the Rolling Stones, and the Beach Boys.

But, like in most households, it was the Beatles who ruled. My sister was an original Beatlemaniac, starting with the band's debut in America on the Ed Sullivan Show. She scooped up every record they released, and her love for George Harrison was real.

Imagine Debra's horror to discover I'd gotten hold of her Beatle albums and scrawled my name on them with a magic marker. Totally defaced the covers with "Dominic" in thick, black ink. I wasn't trying to be a jerk—I just felt like they were an important part of my life, and that was, I guess, how six-year-old me showed it.

They say our earliest attachment to music stays with us our entire lives. That's why people never seem to give up the songs and artists popular during their high school years, and why oldies radio stations still do remarkably well in the ratings.

My attachment goes beyond that; I actually still have, somewhere in a box in the basement, those old 45s. Scratched up and beat to hell, but I've got 'em, passed down to me by my sis.

I'll even go so far as to say it was my love of the Beatles that led me to a career in radio. Honestly, if I hadn't developed that affection for the band, I'd probably be an architect today.

Yet I knew my dad, the ol' sarge, did not approve. If I ever listened to music, it was in my room with the door closed. He would not, perhaps *could* not, endorse that lifestyle.

Which leads to a turning point in my life.

I was in fourth grade, and we were living in Northern Italy, where my dad was stationed at an American Air Force base. Occasionally I'd wander into the tiny store on the base, the base exchange, referred to as the BX. They had a smattering of albums for sale, and I remember my excitement upon seeing a handful of Beatle albums I hadn't inherited/stolen from Debra.

But I also knew it would be a long time before I ever got my hands on one. My meager allowance wouldn't cover the cost of an album, and my dad would never let me spend my money on trashy rock albums, anyway. So I eyed them for a minute, reverently placed them back in the bin, and moved on.

A few days later, Dad came into my room, holding a shopping bag. He held it out to me and said, "Here. I know you've been wanting this." Then he turned and left.

I reached into the bag and pulled out a copy of *"Sgt. Pepper's Lonely Hearts Club Band."*

It was so long ago, so I don't remember if I cried. But I know I was stunned. I turned that album over and over in my hands, studying the incredible artwork on the front cover, then flipping it over and reading the lyrics printed on the backside—a first in the rock world.

Then I put the album on my puny little turntable and fell into the Beatles' psychedelic masterpiece.

It's been more than half a century, but I still have that album today. In fact, I've pulled it out of the cabinet where it normally sits, and I'm looking at it as I write these words. The cover has some minor scuffing, and the disc itself is certainly not pristine—I was a kid, for God's sake; I didn't know to treat a vinyl LP with any sort of delicate touch. But overall, given its age, I'd say it has held up quite well.

It's somewhat rare, too, since it was pressed by the German record label, Odeon—but no amount of money could ever tempt me to sell it.

I've moved more than 15 times since *Sgt. Pepper* fell into my hands, and it has traveled with me across every mile.

Now and then, I'll think back to that moment, sitting in my room in Desenzano, Italy, when I received the gift. And sometimes it makes me think about the power of a gift in general.

What happened to gift giving? When did it morph from an expression of love and appreciation into more of an obligation?

Birthdays and holidays roll around and you're overcome with pressure; pressure to not only find a gift, but the *right* gift. You may not feel judged by the person on the receiving end, but you sure as shit get judged by others who also bought a gift. Did yours measure up? Was it thoughtful? Was it expensive enough?

True, in ancient times, gifts had an entirely different meaning. They often were used to buy influence and form alliances. Many times, the gifts themselves were flesh and blood.

At least we've evolved beyond that.

Even so, if you ask most people about gifts, they'll either reference a holiday or birthday or anniversary—which implies, even subtly, an obligation. Think about Christmas, where you receive an unexpected gift from someone and you haven't purchased anything for them. The stress level shoots up and you rush out to find something.

Don't get me wrong, I'm not bashing any of this. I'm just highlighting our usual association with the word in order to make a point. We clearly have commercialized the idea of gifts.

The very definition of the word makes it clear there should be no expectation of reciprocation. In an idealized world, we don't give a gift expecting something in return.

So I think back to that day when I was not yet even ten years old, and my father walked into my room and shocked the ever-loving shit out of me with a gift that couldn't have been more surprising and unexpected. That was the very epitome of a gift, and it honestly altered the path of my life.

I also think about how our perception of a gift has

become tied to physical items. We're a consumer society, we buy and sell things. Hey, that's how we pay for our shelter and food and toys. And exchanging physical items has become our go-to for acknowledging events. If you go to a birthday party, it's natural to hand over a bottle of wine or gift card or something you know they'll enjoy.

But consider the gifts with no association to a holiday or date and likely don't involve a physical item. There's hardly any emphasis on these gifts anymore, and I think that's a shame.

Yes, the "*Sgt. Pepper*" album inside the shopping bag was a traditional gift, although it wasn't my birthday. It could fall into the "just because" category.

The real kindness, though—what moved it into a different category of gift—wasn't the actual vinyl collection of songs. It was more about what the gesture *represented*, symbolizing my father's loosening of his strict military style. This was the principal power figure in my life communicating a change in our relationship. Even at my young age, I understood on some level the shift that had just taken place. I think it's the main reason I stood there with my mouth hanging open as I first glimpsed the contents of that bag.

We're in a position to provide gifts all the time. Not the physical trinkets, but the gestures. Our actions can often create more of a positive reaction than anything that comes with a bow on it. Those actions can *move* someone, to the point where it shifts your relationship. Sounds very woo-woo, but it's true.

Sadly, I think the emphasis on physical gift exchanges has reduced the frequency of these subtle, yet powerful, interactions. For a variety of reasons, we default to giving a *thing*: it's often easier, there's peer pressure to participate, and it's something that's now just expected.

And, to be frank, not every gift can be of the kind I described with my dad. We don't always have those opportunities. Many times, the bottle of wine is just the best choice.

But when you do have the right opportunity, it's good for the soul to take advantage, to make the gesture.

It's a gift for both people involved in the transaction.

Chapter 21
A Remedy for Sadness

I am a college dropout. I got halfway through, finished my sophomore year, then never went back. I was already a father, working full time, and I honestly didn't see how a degree in communications would help me any more than my natural stick-to-it-tiveness.

We could throw down the gloves and spar for hours about how many young people should attend college. My opinion on the subject once got me banned from a school.

I used to give 12 to 15 presentations a year at schools, educating them on writing and speaking. I loved it. But I'll never forget the time I came off the stage at one particular middle school to find the principal waiting for me. She had a scowl on her face, and I couldn't understand why. The presentation had gone well, with the kids thoroughly engaged and the energy level high.

But she wanted to chat with me about the Q&A session that wrapped up the assembly, which I'd thought was also terrific. The problem, it turned out, was my A to one kid's Q. He'd asked what college I'd graduated from and what degree I'd obtained.

Of course, I was honest. I told him—and the room full of kids—that I'd not finished college, and how it might not be for everybody. Then we moved on to the next question.

The principal coldly informed me that, at this school, they fully expected EVERY SINGLE CHILD to attend college. Nothing short of 100% participation. That, she told me, was the goal, and she wasn't thrilled that I'd suggested college life may not be for everyone.

It was the last time I was ever invited to speak at that school.

Look, she can lead in whatever manner she sees fit. I'm sure she's a remarkable administrator, and I have no doubt she cares a great deal for her students.

But suggesting that 100% of kids should attend college is one of the most foolish things I've ever heard. If you're about to perform open heart surgery on me, then yes, I hope you have tons of formal education.

However, a plumber recently re-plumbed my entire house, replacing every single pipe. Do you think I gave a shit if he had a college degree? Oh, and he left my house with a check for $26,000.

How stupid are we that we force kids to attend college when we—or they—have no idea what they want to do with their lives? And just so you know, that plumber makes about $150k a year. Not bad for a guy without a dime of college loan debt.

If you couldn't tell, this is a subject that fires me up —but it's actually *not* the point of this chapter.

The point is education in general. And, specifically, how it can lift us up from the doldrums.

When I was in high school, I read T. H. White's classic "*The Once and Future King*", and just re-read it a couple of years ago for fun. In its pages, I stumbled across a line uttered by the wizard Merlyn. It stopped me cold. I went back and read it again, then again.

In chapter 21, Merlyn tells a very young Arthur, long before the boy becomes a king:

"*The best thing for being sad is to learn something. That is the only thing that never fails.*"
He adds: "*Learn why the world wags and what wags it. That is the only thing which the mind can never exhaust, never alienate, never be tortured by, never fear or distrust, and never dream of regretting.*"

For years, I've realized I'm somebody who knows a little bit about a lot of things. I may not be a super whiz at any one thing, but I'm proud to say I have little snippets of knowledge over a wide swath of topics. I prefer it that way.

And while I have no college degree hanging on my wall—which, as we've learned from at least one school principal, makes me a complete and total loser—I also didn't stop learning the day I left school. Plenty of people put in their 12 years of public school and maybe four years of college, and then they shut off the tap. They pretty much stop learning.

I've encountered so many people—usually men—who almost proudly proclaim, "I haven't read a book since college." Like it's a badge of honor.

Look, "education" isn't just something you get at an institution of higher learning. Education should be something we strive for daily. I don't care if it's YouTube videos, reading books, taking an art class on the side, or even just picking up some tools and figuring things out as you go along.

Never. Stop. Learning.

I gave a lot of thought to what Merlyn said to young Arthur, how learning is the antidote for sadness. Clearly, if a person is battling depression, it will take more than just learning how to crochet to lift up their mental health. For anyone who is chronically depressed, I would urge therapy.

But when it comes to a baseline sense of happiness and fulfillment, Merlyn has got it going on. Consistently charging your mind with learning new snippets of information or taking on the task of learning new skills does more than just keep the doldrums at bay. Studies support the idea that actively learning also has an impact on what's known as your cognitive reserve, which many believe is a key to withstanding various age-related issues, such as dementia.

Let It Be Good

Use it or lose it, some might say.

Along these lines, I had an interesting discussion with an acquaintance who used all of her free time rewatching her favorite television series on a streaming service. By this point, she'd seen every episode—and there were more than 100 of them—no fewer than 30 times each. She estimated she rewatched two to three every single day.

That's a minimum of 3,000 times she has plopped onto the couch and ingested the same dialogue and canned laughter. She proudly claimed she could recite every episode, line by line, as each character spoke the words.

When she saw how perplexed I was at this lifestyle choice, she remarked: "It's my comfort zone."

Is it really, though? Is that a comfort zone, or simply compulsive behavior cloaked as comfort? Or would a psychologist tell me there's no difference between the two?

Here's how I look at it: Even a conservative estimate of 15 episodes a week, times 23 minutes per episode, comes out to around 300 *hours* a year. That's 300 hours rewatching the same things, over and over, the equivalent of 12 full days.

Damn, that's an awful lot of mindless time in the name of relaxing in a "comfort zone."

My mind can't help but think of how much new information this person could be ingesting, how many fresh neural pathways could be stimulated in her brain. Even if she split the time in half, that would be 150 hours devoted to learning something new, rather than reciting the same lines with Ross and Rachel.

I can already hear the argument: *Dom, this book is supposed to be about living a satisfied life. What if watching my favorite show over and over is what satisfies me?*

I'm no dummy; I know trying to convince someone to shut off the sitcom and pick up a book is a losing battle in most cases. No fantasies here about convincing the masses to do *anything*.

But, to be blunt, I've never really given a damn about stirring the masses. I'm excited about influencing a few people to make significant changes to improve their well-being and to set them up for a more satisfied life down the road. I will never win a battle against pizza and TV. Hell, *I* like pizza and TV.

I've just learned over time that true satisfaction is something with a long tail, not immediate gratification. I live a curious life, and I truly believe it's the superior framework for ultimate happiness.

What can you learn in the next 30 days?

And how much happier do you anticipate it will make you?

Chapter 22
The Positive Password

Brian had an argument one morning with his wife, just as he was leaving for work. By the time he arrived at the office, his emotions had meandered this way and that, alternating between anger, frustration, and, finally, regret.

Sitting at his desk, he logged on to his computer and stared at the message on his screen. The message that produces groans from many of us.

His company's security department demanded that employees change their password every 45 days, and the pop-up notice now informed him that today was the day.

It's bad enough when you're having a *good* day, having to dream up yet another password and getting that irritating reminder that YOU CAN'T REUSE OLD PASSWORDS. If you're like me, you have two dozen passwords for the two dozen (or more) sites and applications where you need them. We certainly can't remember what we've used where.

I have a document I keep updated with all my various passwords, and I keep *that* in its own password-protected file. But it's still a hassle, every damned time. Not only do I have to come up with the new combination of letters, numbers, and symbols, but I have to remember to update the master file.

Brian was *not* having a good morning, and the last thing he needed at that moment was a command to invent a new freaking password.

That's when the idea hit.

He pulled the keyboard toward him and quickly typed in his new password:

ForgiveMe&LoveAmy.

With a flourish, he banged the return key and the new password was saved. And for the next six weeks, every time he logged on he got a quick reminder that he should be more forgiving of himself and more loving to his wife.

It didn't take him long to realize how powerful this was. When another 45 days went by, he changed his password to:

Save$LoveAmy.

Brian had created a ritual, one he was guaranteed to follow through with every day. He put into motion a system for improving his life, visually reminding himself of two things at a time that could positively impact his world.

It's one of those life hacks that's so damned simple that you probably think, "Why the hell didn't I think of this?" We all grumble whenever we have to change our passwords, and we've almost run out of clever ways to incorporate our dog's name or children's birthdays. Why not use this obligatory task to subtly better ourselves?

It's not like we don't stare at screens all day.

After reading Brian's story, I spent some time thinking about the concept. Yeah, we come up with one or two things that we could stand to improve about ourselves. But it dawned on me that since we require so many of the damned things on a daily basis, we could tailor each one.

Your office computer's password might contain something about your profession you'd like to improve. Maybe a reminder to be nicer to the people who stop by your desk, or to finish one project before starting another.

At home, maybe your streaming passwords could be something about your relationship, or perhaps some words of clarity when it comes to your parenting responsibilities.

Your social media passwords could remind you to not take things too seriously. We all know social media algorithms are designed to suck you into arguments and disagreements; maybe your password could short-circuit that.

What if you couldn't log on to Facebook without reminding yourself to *LightenUp!* The rest of us might never again have to read a political rant.

Ah, well, a boy can dream.

You could use other passwords to target your health. What about *Walk10000?* Maybe you work on your life skills by typing in *BePresent!* Or *ListenMore!*

Six weeks of positive impressions, followed by six more, then six more.

The definition of a *mantra* has expanded over the years. It's often associated with spiritual or magical powers, including words or sounds used in prayer and meditation. People and companies today, however, often use it as shorthand for a pledge of sorts, a way of defining a particular rule of conduct.

Regardless of how you define it, one of the underlying principles is to repeat the word or phrase in order to keep it in the forefront of your mind, where it can hopefully guide your thoughts and actions.

Well, if you think about it, what Brian came up with —and what many people have adopted as their own—is a sort of digital mantra, one you have no choice but to repeat again and again, every time you deal with one of those damned screens.

I know this concept has staying power. When I first wrote a blog post about it nearly ten years ago, several people enthusiastically replied.

Three years later, a couple of these people got back in

touch to say they were still implementing the strategy, finding new ways to incorporate positive passwords into an otherwise boring routine.

Since there's a lot of power in gratitude, perhaps your first new password could be *ThanksBrian!*

Chapter 23
Satisfaction

Plenty of people have had profound thoughts on the idea of satisfaction, either because they have it, they long for it, or they can never seem to get it.

Salvador Dali said he sometimes had so much satisfaction that he feared he might die of an overdose.

Khalil Gibran said to look back upon your life and be satisfied is "to live twice."

And Norman Vincent Peale, who wrote the bestselling book "The Power of Positive Thinking", encouraged us to learn to like ourselves. As he said, since we spend so much time with ourselves, we should at least get satisfaction out of the relationship.

Of course, Mick Jagger and the Stones went to #1 by bitching that they couldn't get no satisfaction. Color me skeptical; I think they were satisfied out of their minds throughout the 1960s and 70s.

It would be easy for me to ask if you're satisfied, but during the nearly two years I spent writing this book, I realized you may not know the answer. I'm not sure *I* know the answer, either. I've attempted to sculpt my once-haphazard life into a shape where today I can say I'm happy—but am I *satisfied*?

In the chapter titled "Two Pins From Perfect", I made it sound like I could never be satisfied, *a la* Jagger, and that I would always strive for more. That sounds like something philosopher and historian Yuval Noah Harari talked about, basically proposing that we can never be satisfied because pleasure only leads us to chase *more* pleasure, so that we crave more without ever being satisfied.

Like hamsters on a satisfaction wheel. Damn, that sounds miserable.

Somewhere, somehow, there's a creamy middle we all strive for. A place where you may be still pushing for more, and yet ultimately happy with where you are. That Goldilocks zone from Chapter 18, perhaps.

Many people place a priority on their personal relationships above all other components when it comes to their satisfaction scale. They could be killing it in the professional world, but a void in their love life or family dynamic is enough to temper any feelings of success.

This is such a difficult matter to analyze, a swirling, chaotic combination of factors that not only aligns differently for everyone, but is easily influenced by outside forces. In fact, the very definition of a relationship is "the state of being interrelated." You may have all your ducks in a row, but the person you're attempting to partner with is . . . well, a mess. Their issues most certainly become *your* issues.

Often a match made in heaven takes you on a detour through hell. I speak from personal experience—and *I* was the conductor.

I married very young, and, like many young couples in that situation, we discovered we weren't right for each other. After ten years of marriage, I was single again. And in almost no time at all, I met someone who was an absolute catch. Couldn't believe my luck, really.

And that must've played a part in what happened next. Because I'd been through a tough stretch, I suppose I didn't trust that things *could* be golden. I held back. I couldn't devote my full attention to this new partner, whom I'll call Kay. I was sure—even if only subconsciously—that it, too, must end.

Well, it did. Because of me. I let a remarkable life partner walk away because I was still emotionally naïve.

So in that sense, could I have been satisfied that I'd found 'the one,' or whatever tag you want to assign? Yes. Perhaps I could've been happy for the rest of my life in this relationship. Kay was someone who checked every box, and yet I let her down. Her satisfaction was, in this case, directly affected by me. I couldn't grasp what I had, either because I was still reeling from the turbulence of my divorce, or because I simply didn't have enough experience. Probably both.

Finding satisfaction in a relationship is, I'm

convinced, a matter of both time and space. Where are you in *time*, and in what *place* in your life?

It's like runners in a 1500-meter race. They start at staggered points on the track, and for the first lap or two they stay in their lane, separated by distance. They're both running the same race, but until they slip down into that low lane together, it's as if they're *not* in the same race.

We may be in a good space, where we can be happy and satisfied, but if our potential partner is still in another lane, it's tough going for both of us.

Kay was ready for our race to sync up; I was unprepared.

Years later, I *did* meet someone who was in the same time and space. As I write this, we've been married for six years. But it didn't work for us until we'd put in several laps around the track and wound up in the same lane.

There's an old saying that you shouldn't rely on another person for your happiness. Make yourself happy, find someone else who has done the same, and support each other as you make your way through life. Just don't count on *them* for your happiness.

It's a hard concept for some to accept. Books, greeting cards, Hollywood films, and the distorted reality we see daily on social media have us convinced our happiness—indeed, the *satisfaction* we're exploring in this book—is directly tied to another individual. Some call it romantic. Others say it's a toxic mindset.

I reject both extreme labels.

Relying on another person to make you happy and satisfied is simply insecurity. You may have been through a traumatic relationship in your past and you're now hoping for someone you can lean on to make you happy. Psychologically, I get it.

So what happens when *that* person lets you down? Or what happens when they suddenly have their *own* happiness issues to deal with? Are they supposed to supply the fuel for both of you?

Of course, we all experience tough stretches where we rely on our partner to help us get through. That's normal and even expected. But to place the burden on someone else to make sure you are *always* happy? That's not love. That's codependency. And truly unfair to another person.

The strongest couples I've ever known are the ones who have made their individual ways in life and chosen to finish the race together. Not because they *have* to, but because they choose to.

If you're struggling with your personal life, you have my empathy. Been there. Been through gloomy times, times where I wasn't sure I'd ever pull out. Just know that focusing on your happiness without the crutch of another person is a great exit ramp off the highway to hell. It doesn't mean walling yourself off from love or companionship, but it does mean learning to be happy in your own skin, which—surprise!—will make you attractive to someone else. It just works that way.

And if it takes more time than you expected? So

what? Better to put in the time and end up with a better partner.

And if it never works out? Then at least you've invested years into finding your own happiness. I'm a big believer that it's way better to be happy alone than to be miserable in a subpar relationship.

Look, I'm not a therapist, although I do fancy myself something of a relationship expert. I've been through enough good and enough bad to counsel anyone on what they may be experiencing.

No offense, but someone who met their spouse when they were 16 and have now been inseparable for 40 years? I think that's spectacular. Cheers to you. Well done.

But I don't think that makes you a relationship expert. I think it makes you an expert on that ONE person. Someone who has only driven Fords their entire life could write a book on Fords and I'd be impressed—but I'm not going to trust anything they say about Toyotas, Chevys, or Porsches.

Relationship experts are people who have been in more than one.

Just my opinion.

Now, having said that, I'm clearly NOT an expert on careers and should be the last person you consult.

Because this is the other area of satisfaction that carries a lot of weight for people. If they're unhappy in their job, it does bleed over into the other parts of their world.

Let It Be Good

I've essentially done one job my whole life. I've been a radio geek since age 16, and, unless I get shown the door before September 2027, I'll hit 50 years in the industry. It's all I've known, other than my writing.

So no double-standard here. I could advise you all day on relationships. On jobs? I've got a long, but incomplete, resume.

But here's what I *do* know. Most of us want to feel productive, and we certainly want to feel appreciated. Are you in a field where both things happen?

On my radio show, I'm constantly asking callers what they do for a living. For me, it's interesting to discover the wide variety of occupations out there, some of which I find fascinating.

A woman once told me her job was to drive pee around town. When someone left a urine sample at a clinic, her job was to pick it up and drive it to the lab. So at any given time, while she was listening to the radio show, she had dozens of beakers filled with human pee.

Never thought about someone doing that, have you?

I also ask the callers if they enjoy what they're doing. More than half say yes, which makes me happy. I adore my job, always have, and it breaks my heart to find people who groan each day when they fall out of bed, dreading the day ahead. What a tragic way to live.

If you're in a place like that, what can you do to find satisfaction?

I doubt the complete answer can be found in a book. I know the self-help section at the store is packed with gurus who believe they can guide you, and perhaps some can.

But career satisfaction is another one of those delicate balances. Not just because it involves finding a job in which you're skilled, but because it's so damned dependent upon the people around you. I've done basically the same job for decades, but I can tell you the people who have surrounded me have had almost everything to do with my happiness levels.

Seems almost unfair. We work so hard to learn our craft, and put in so many hours improving through the years. But we're a social society, and that social element is interwoven into our career path as much as it is into our personal/friend path.

I have to believe this is why so many people demand to work from home. Yes, the pandemic of 2020 started the ball rolling. But once people got a taste of avoiding Surly Sue in the next cubicle, it was a eureka moment. I'm sure there are studies backing it up, but common sense alone would tell me that people like what they do—they just may not like the people around them.

And, to be fair, while you may find some of your coworkers difficult to be around, they could easily feel the same way about you.

I wrote a piece a few years ago about the Career Venn Diagram. The overlapping circles, right? Well, in this case, I said the best career for you was the one where

Let It Be Good

three categories overlapped. The simplified version went like this:

One, is it something you enjoy?
Two, is it something you're good at?
Three, is it something that can pay you a good salary?

Argue if you must about these, but you'll never, ever see me coach young people to simply "follow your passion." There are a shitload of people who have followed their passion all the way to a bedroom in their parents' basement.

I subscribe to the theory that you find the intersection of those three circles and *bring your passion along with you*.

But lately, especially upon writing this book, I've realized there's a fourth circle in my Career Venn Diagram:

Are you surrounded by people who make the work place enjoyable?

There's dangerous footing here. If you're overly sensitive and need perfect coworkers at all times, then I maintain *you're* probably the nightmare.

We've all worked with people who make the job miserable. In that case, you either need to find a way to work away from them or—gulp—find another job. I know, easier said than done, and not a step many are willing to take.

Or you find a way to not let them affect you as much. This could be a discussion with your life partner or with a career coach or even a professional therapist.

It's just that career happiness can often be so important to a satisfied life. The *most* important? Well, people are different. It's certainly vital to me. When I'm happy at work, it's like the rising tide that raises all boats. Every other part of my life seems to improve.

Whether it's a personal relationship or your work environment, how do you really define *satisfaction*? Is it being deliriously happy every day? Or is it more of just a baseline contentment?

Over beers one day, a very dear friend once told me: "Everyone is unhappy."

And perhaps there's a sliver of truth in that. We're probably all toting around some lingering or simmering disappointment, some kernel of unhappiness that stubbornly hangs on. To my way of thinking, it's all about how much that kernel defines you or influences your behavior.

Again, people are wired differently. Some need complete perfection or their stress level spikes. Others are more chill than a sloth. Genetics, probably.

I'll tell you what has worked wonders for me, and you might think it's stupid.

I go for a walk.

Laugh, if you must. But walking outside has been a

critical part of my life for the last 20 years. If more than two days go by without it, I get antsy.

It's not just the physical element. It's the time to think. It's getting out of work, out of the house, away from my normal surroundings, and detaching from the usual stress.

We know about the release of endorphins from physical exercise, the hormones that help to regulate our stress levels. I'm a believer. But I'm also a disciple of the distancing that goes on, both physically and metaphorically. My walks are when I do the bulk of my important thinking.

My prescription for anyone who's able to do it is to invest 30 to 45 minutes a day, at the very least. No outside stimuli, no podcast or audiobook, no talking to a friend on the phone. Just walking and thinking. I know many will say it's boring—well, LEARN TO BE BORED, goddammit. You're not five. You should be able to be alone with your thoughts for 45 minutes.

I promise you, this is where you'll build a foundation of personal satisfaction. It's where you'll realize how often you blow shit out of proportion, and where you find solutions to minor personal conflicts before they expand into real problems that siphon your happiness.

And, like any habit, the more you do it, the more you'll long to do it.

So then, the bottom line: Are you satisfied?

Are you happy with your career? Are you happy with

your personal life? Do your hobbies bring you joy? If you have no hobbies, that could be one of the problems.

I think we've been trained in the last few years that everything must be perfect. We're constantly shown pictures of people living a glamorous, sun-splashed life—and the implication is that if you don't have *this*, you must be unsatisfied.

Don't fall for that bullshit. Never dance to someone else's tune. If you find yourself judging your satisfaction by how much crap you can accumulate, or how many *amaaazziiing* vacations you can take in the Mediterranean—well, just be aware that most of us fall into that trap for a while. Human nature.

We only have so much time to figure it out. Please don't waste it. In a movie called "Summer Wishes, Winter Dreams," a character named Harry explains it this way:

"Listen, they give you a cupful of time. You drink it or you spill it on the floor. You think time cares what you do?"

Or anyone else in the world, for that matter.

Have you surrounded yourself with the people who will contribute to your happiness and satisfaction? I know I've held onto friendships too long. You probably have, as well.

I'm convinced the best thing you can do is jettison the assholes in your life—and those can be personal relationships or professional relationships. John Waters, the actor, writer, and filmmaker, is often quoted as saying:

Real wealth is never having to spend time with assholes.

What he actually said, in a commencement speech he gave at the Rhode Island School of Design, was:

I'm rich. I don't mean money-wise. I mean that I have figured out how to never be around assholes at any time in my personal and professional life. That's *rich.*

The paraphrased version is short and sweet, but either way, the point is the same. The people around us have way more power than you think. They're influencing your actions and your behavior to a significant degree, and often the best move you can make is to excise them from your sphere. It's not always easy, but the payoff is worth it.

I've done that in both arenas and have found it's like coming up for air after being submerged for ages. On the radio show, we used to call it "pruning your garden." It's time for you to bust out the garden implements.

So the ultimate takeaway from this chapter is:

Break your world down into tiny, bite-sized portions, and audit each one. I promise it will be an awakening for you. You'll soon realize what's really important to you and what isn't. And if it doesn't fit the social media "ideal," so much the better.

Sending you best wishes for a contented, satisfied walk through life.

Chapter 24
Closing Thoughts

It must take an extraordinary amount of patience to work in IT support. I would imagine for every real/complex problem they solve, IT helpers must put up with a dozen people who simply need to reboot their computer.

Or just plug it in. A tech support pro told me it works out that way on more calls than you'd think. That's why IT people use acronyms like PICNIC to describe someone who's not very sharp when it comes to computers: Problem In Chair, Not In Computer.

Or they'll log the issue as an ID 10 T. You should be able to stare at that for a moment and figure it out.

What's frustrating for the rest of us is when they're right, and all we needed to do was turn the damned thing off and then back on again. Seems like complicated technology should require more than that, don't you think? That's probably why we didn't think of such a simple solution, because the system itself is so freaking *complex*.

How could the fix possibly be as simple as turning it off and on? It's almost like the joke is on us. And I guess it is.

But really, the same fix works for us. I know it sounds lame, but it's funny how often we just need a good reboot.

As I looked back over the chapters in this book, it dawned on me that that's pretty much what I'm observing and/or recommending. Given the way we're built, and because the human race has such a high opinion of itself, we don't like to think our problems can be solved or mitigated by unplugging, stepping back, and then wading back in with a new perspective.

In a way, that could explain why some people are reluctant to explore therapy. They believe their brain is so intricate and so *evolved* that something as simple as sitting down and hashing out an issue could never be what solves the problem. And yet, therapy is a fancy way of rebooting our thought processes. And I mean that in a complimentary way.

Mental health professionals claim more than 70% of adults deal with stress severe enough to impact not just their mental health, but to also have detrimental effects on their physical well-being, too. Stress, to put it bluntly, is a killer.

Well, some will tell you that stress is a product of the importance we place on something, often arbitrarily. To a certain extent, nothing is actually important unless we *tell ourselves* it's important. Granted, when other people are involved, we should certainly take them into consideration.

Let It Be Good

But it's hard to deny that the bulk of stress keeping us up at night, or causing us to binge eat or drink, or creating a physical breakdown, is brought on by artificial deadlines and random levels of importance *we* place on things.

I'm not telling you to chill out to the point you're a zombie, or that you should blow off all your responsibilities. But I *am* suggesting you slip out of the fast lane as much as possible. Many people have a goal of decluttering their home—well, why not declutter your mind? Try eliminating as many dots on your calendar as possible. That's a hard experiment—at first. The more you get into the habit of saying no and leaving time to breathe, the easier it will be to make it a priority.

And you'll be amazed at how *un*important many of those seemingly important items turn out to be.

I don't know what our factory settings are when it comes to stress and how it relates to our happiness and satisfaction. Clearly, each person is built differently. But just as a reset button works on everything from video game systems to phones to laptops to streaming devices, a personal reset button works on every human being.

As long as we're willing to push it.

Remember what I said in the introduction: I don't write to teach. I write to learn. For a while now, I've wondered about the divide between happiness and satisfaction.

Writing "*Let It Be Good*" showed me so many components to the satisfaction equation that the entire writing process turned into something of a personal master class.

One thing I've learned for sure: happiness is fleeting. It's very much baked into a specific moment in time, which is why you can be happy at 8 A.M. and unhappy at 2 P.M. We're triggered by isolated incidents that have power over our happiness, like it or not. And while the self-help book industry is fueled by teaching you how to be happy—and, in the process, generates $10 billion in sales annually—I think that's a fool's errand.

Be unhappy when you need to be. That's fine, and it defines you as human.

In early 2025, university researchers from Canada and Australia released the results of a study that found the relentless pursuit of happiness can produce the opposite effect. Putting maximum effort into consistently chasing happiness ends up making people miserable.

They described it as a snowball effect, where the more you try to make yourself feel happy, the more you're depleting the mental energy you need to do the things in life that actually make you feel good, such as being active, being productive, and solving problems.

As one researcher said, putting an enormous amount of energy into finding happiness drains your energy reserves, and instead of cleaning the house later that day—which would give you a sense of accomplishment, which aids happiness—you plop onto the couch and scroll through social media.

And we already know the effect that has on the human brain.

But satisfaction . . .

This is purely one man's opinion, formulated over years of a trial-and-error life, but satisfaction is arriving at a place of acceptance. Not necessarily acceptance that you've achieved the best in life that you're capable of, but that you're at least on the right path.

Acceptance requires honesty. Being honest about your efforts and about your expectations. Being honest about the place you're in, which includes where you are in life and—importantly—who you've chosen to take this ride with you, both personally and professionally.

I still have goals I've yet to achieve. But am I satisfied with my life?

Yes. And I can't say that was the case even a few years ago.

The reboots I've done have smoothed out a lot of the bumps. The personal and professional choices I've made have played a major part. And maybe just finally learning what it means to be satisfied, because I'm not sure we truly understand it until we reach a certain stage of life.

Although it's been falsely attributed to many other people, it was Dr. Bob Moorehead who wrote in "The Paradox of Our Age":

We've learned how to make a living, but not a life.

I've finally learned how to pay attention to the simple insights strewn along our path. We ignore them in our haste when we're young, we overlook them in our prime earning years because we're focused on the 'big picture'—whatever that is—and we perhaps carry a negative bias about the power of the *simple*.

Including the simplicity of a personal reboot.

In the folder I created while writing this book, I logged at least one hundred of these simple insights. I chose two dozen for publication. That doesn't make the others any less potent; in fact, each one holds a lot of power for me.

You have your own life lessons, your own experiences. I hope you shut off the world for a bit and swim in those simple insights. You'll see how they, too, can be a gift. How they can demonstrate to you how powerful *good* can be—without the need to be perfect.

Find your happiness, no matter how fleeting, and watch over time how it can lay the foundation for a satisfied life.

Dom Testa
March 3, 2025

Also by Dom Testa

Non-fiction

Domino On Your Radio: Unlikely Tales From an Introvert on the Air

The Color of Your Dreams: Publish Your Damn Book Already

The Mindbender Book series

The Billy B. Good Fun Facts and Trivia Snacks series

* * *

Fiction

The Eric Swan spy thriller series

The Galahad young adult sci-fi series (written as Tyber North)

The Buster Blank middle grade series (written as Buster Blank)

Wednesday, and Other Dark Tales (written as Harlan Plumber)

* * *

Discover them all at DomTestaBooks.com.

www.ingramcontent.com/pod-product-compliance
Lightning Source LLC
Chambersburg PA
CBHW032038290426
44110CB00012B/850